P9-DDU-288

3/04

Historical Atlases of South Asia,
Central Asia, and the Middle East™

A HISTORICAL ATLAS OF

AZERBAIJAN

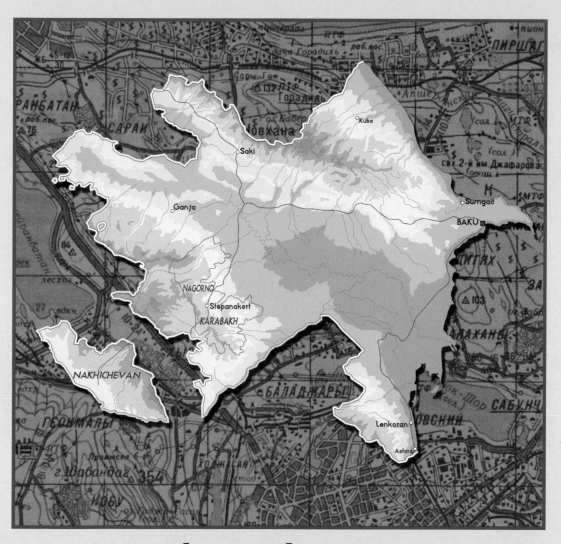

Sherri Liberman

The Rosen Publishing Group, Inc., New York

Published in 2004 by The Rosen Publishing Group, Inc.
29 East 21st Street, New York, NY 10010

First Edition

Library of Congress Cataloging-in-Publication Data

Liberman, Sherri.
A historical atlas of Azerbaijan / Sherri Liberman.
    p. cm. — (Historical atlases of South Asia, Central Asia, and the Middle East)
Summary: Maps and text chronicle the history of the former Soviet republic of
Azerbaijan, located in the Caucasus Mountains at a crossroads on the Asian continent.
Includes bibliographical references (p.) and index.
Contents: Prehistory — Ancient empires — The birth of Islam — Medieval empires —
Russian imperialism — The Soviet era — Birth of a republic.
ISBN 0-8239-4497-2
1. Azerbaijan — History — Maps for children. 2. Azerbaijan — Maps for children — .
[1. Azerbaijan — History. 2. Atlases.] I. Title. II. Series.
G2164.41.S1L5 2004
911'.4754 — dc22

2003055019

Manufactured in the United States of America

Cover images: The twelfth-century structure known as the Maiden's Tower of Baku, a
nineteenth-century painting of Peter the Great, czar of Russia from 1721 to 1725, and the
current president of Azerbaijan, Heydar Aliyev, are shown with an eighteenth-century
map of the Russian Empire (background) and a contemporary map of Azerbaijan.

Contents

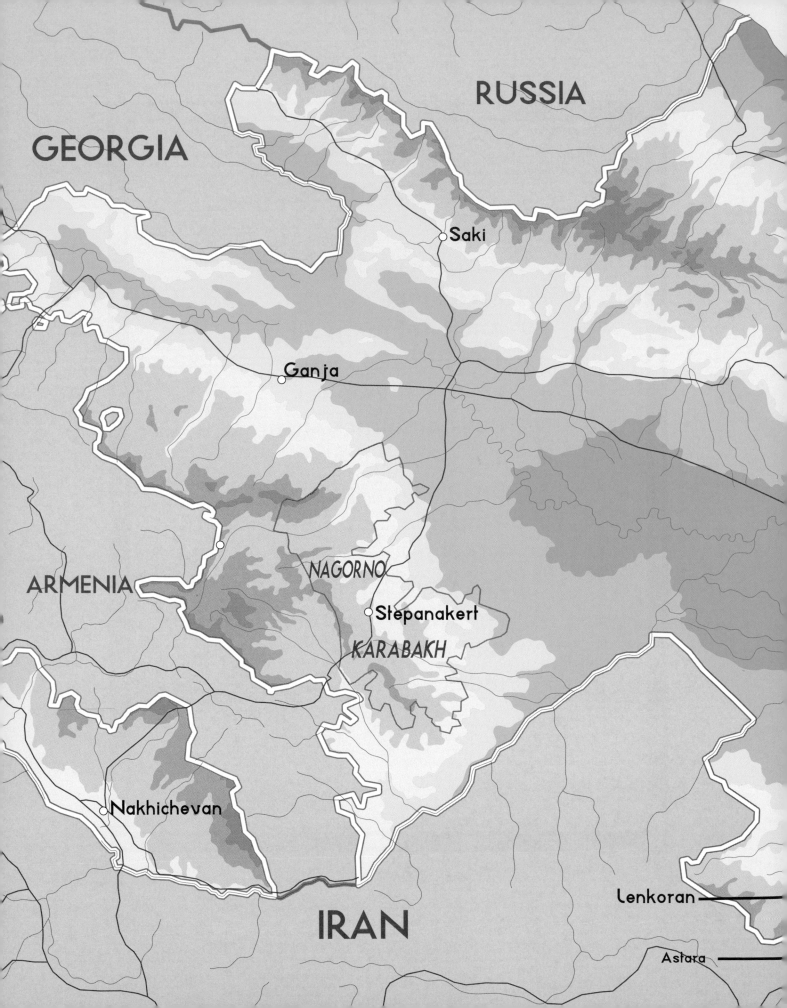

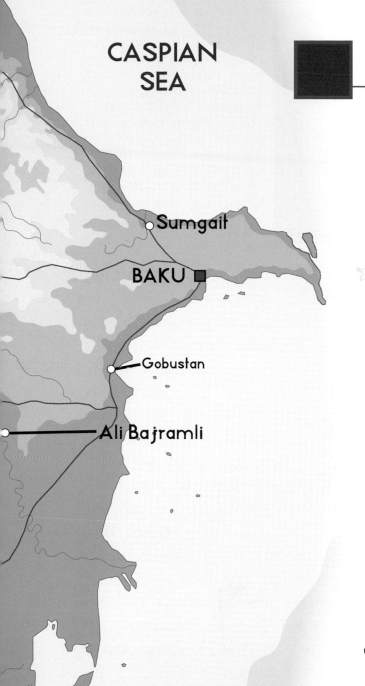

CASPIAN
SEA

Sumgait

BAKU ■

Gobustan

Ali Bajramli

INTRODUCTION

Azerbaijan is known as the Land of Fire. From its earliest inhabitants who huddled by fires in the Caucasus Mountains, to the fire-worshiping temples of Zoroastrians in Baku, Azerbaijan has witnessed a history of changing cultures.

Located on the western shores of the Caspian Sea, today's Republic of Azerbaijan occupies about 33,400 square miles (86,505 square kilometers), roughly the same size as the state of Maine. The former Soviet republics of Georgia and Armenia lie on its western borders, and Iran forms its border to the south, separated by the Araks River and the Talysh Mountains.

Armenia, Azerbaijan, and Georgia are referred to as Caucasia, also known as Transcaucasia, due to their location south of the Caucasus Mountains. The Russian

Azerbaijan is a landlocked nation in Caucasia, a region of Asia that spreads between the Black and Caspian Seas and is divided by the Caucasus Mountains. Formerly a part of the Union of Soviet Socialist Republics (USSR), Azerbaijan regained its independence after the collapse of the Soviet Union in 1991. Primarily populated by Turkic Muslims, Azerbaijan's most widely known conflict exists around Nagorno-Karabakh, an interior region of the country seized by Armenian forces in 1988. Although there has been a cease-fire agreement between Armenia and Azerbaijan since 1994, Azerbaijanis are still trying to reclaim Nagorno-Karabakh, which was once about 16 percent of Azerbaijan. Nagorno-Karabakh is now primarily populated by Armenians.

Fountain Square in Baku, the capital of Azerbaijan, is located on the western shores of the Caspian Sea. The square is a popular area for residents and tourists alike, and it is bordered by a variety of restaurants and shops. Baku has both ancient and modern attractions, including its original fortress walls, the twelfth-century Maiden's Tower, and medieval mosques, palaces, and caravan stations. The oldest written reference to Baku, known as the City of Winds, can be traced back to AD 885.

territory of Dagestan borders Azerbaijan's northern boundary. The majority of Azerbaijanis live in the lowlands formed by Azerbaijan's two major rivers, the Kura and the Araks. These waterways provide irrigation for Azerbaijan's farmland.

Azerbaijan occupies a strategic east-west crossroad on the Asian continent, which attracted many conquerors to the region. Azerbaijan once hosted some of history's fiercest warriors, such as Persia's Cyrus the Great; the Macedonian king Alexander the Great; the Roman general Pompey; and the Mongol rulers Genghis Khan and Timur.

Archaeologists have determined from bone fragments found in Azerbaijan that its earliest inhabitants date from the Stone Age. Petroglyphs, or rock paintings, discovered in the coastal village of Gobustan, for example, give archaeologists clues about an advanced prehistoric civilization in Caucasia. Ethnically and linguistically, modern-day Azerbaijanis are thought to be the descendants of nomadic Turkic tribes that migrated to the region more than 1,000 years ago. Presently Azerbaijan is home to numerous ethnic groups, including Kurds, Jews, Russians, and Armenians, weaving a rich tapestry of culture and traditions.

1 PREHISTORY

The story of human settlement in the region known today as Azerbaijan begins during the Stone Age some 730,000 to 1.5 million years ago. Nomadic hunter-gatherers wandered throughout Caucasia, following the migration routes of animals. These ancient people likely sought refuge in caves nestled into the sides of the mountains. The most famous of these is the Azykh cave, located in Azerbaijan's Nagorno-Karabakh region. It is the largest cave of its kind in the Caucasus.

Inside the Azykh cave, archaeologists have discovered the remnants of stone tools made from quartz, flint, and basalt. This discovery provides evidence that the earliest Azerbaijanis had the intelligence to invent tools for survival.

The favorable climate of the Kuruchai River valley, where the Ayzkh cave is located, attracted bison, deer, and bears, a likely reason why prehistoric people settled there. The earliest Azykh cave dwellers are thought to be related to *Homo habilis*, an ancestor of *Homo sapiens* who lived in East Africa two million years ago. Archaeologists describe these inhabitants as Kuruchai. In 1968, archaeologists discovered a jawbone fragment in the Azykh cave. Scientists determined that it belonged to an eighteen-year-old female

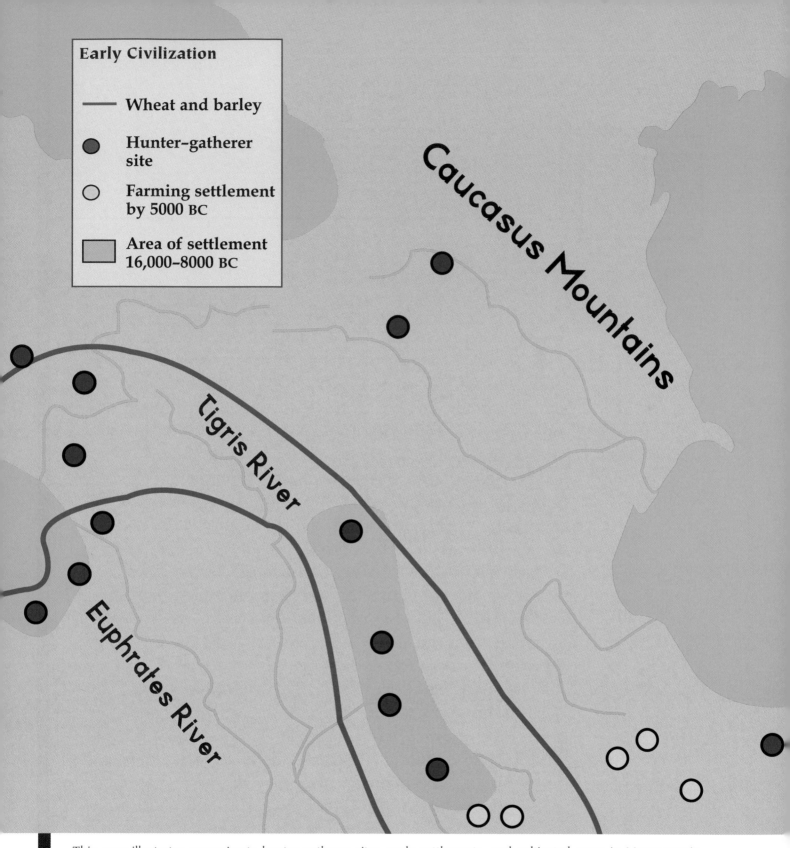

Early Civilization

— Wheat and barley

● Hunter-gatherer site

○ Farming settlement by 5000 BC

▭ Area of settlement 16,000–8000 BC

Caucasus Mountains

Tigris River

Euphrates River

This map illustrates approximate hunter-gatherer sites, early settlements, and cultivated areas in Mesopotamia between 16,000 BC and 5000 BC. The closest region to present-day Azerbaijan that was cultivated is considered part of the Fertile Crescent, or the semicircle of fertile land that stretches from the southeastern coast of the Mediterranean to the Persian Gulf, excluding the desert lands of Saudi Arabia. Based around existing river basins—in this case, the Tigris and the Euphrates Rivers—early civilizations were able to support growing populations and, later, the development of cities and writing.

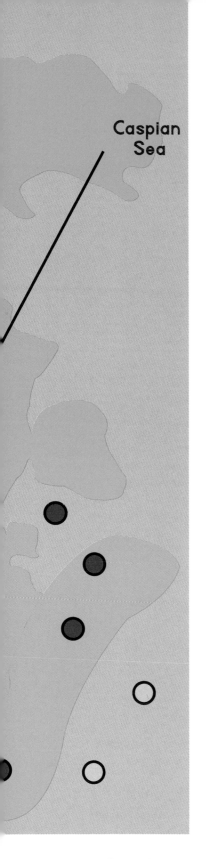

Caspian
Sea

related to a Neanderthal ancestor. The fragment is now thought to be the fourth oldest human artifact ever found in history. Analysis confirmed that it is 350,000 to 400,000 years old.

Evidence of primitive hearths was discovered in the Ayzkh cave, too, which suggests the ability to make fire. Pictures of flames carved into the cave walls also hint at fire worship.

The Apsheron peninsula, a fingerlike projection into the Caspian Sea in northeastern Azerbaijan, shows evidence of Neolithic (10,000–8000 BC) and Bronze Age (5000–4000 BC) culture. The appearance of cart ruts there—parallel grooves cut into rock surfaces—may indicate that carts were used to transport limestone blocks to building sites. Similar cart ruts have been found in the Mediterranean as far away as Greece, Italy, France, and Malta, a small island.

The Apsheron peninsula of northern Azerbaijan, seen here in an aerial photograph, has recently been studied by a number of archaeologists, who revealed its rich history. Thousands of petroglyphs located in a network of caves testify to cultural developments in Azerbaijan dating back at least 10,000 years. The remains of oil fields, Roman graffiti, and several medieval castles also make the area an interesting one for travelers.

Black Sea
today

Caspian Sea
today

Sarmatic Sea
→ to Mediterranean Sea

The Sarmatic Sea was a body of water that may have stretched from present-day Vienna, Austria, to the Tien Shan Mountains of Azerbaijan. Some scientists believe that the Sarmatic may have joined the Black, Azov, Caspian, and Aral Seas about five million years ago. A similar merging of seas may have occurred as recently as 10,000 BC. Scientists now believe that sediment taken from the bottom of the Black Sea reveals earlier periods when the land was dry and then muddy. This observation led them to conclude that the Black Sea was once a smaller freshwater lake. As the climate changed during the last ice age 15,000 years ago, thawed ice increased the level of surrounding seas much like it had millions of years before.

Stone circles and burial mounds have been found in the village of Mardakan, also on the Apsheron peninsula. These megalithic sites may have once served as prehistoric dwellings. Petroglyphs depicting rams were carved on stone surfaces. Archaeologists noticed that the stone circles of Mardakan bore an uncanny resemblance to ones found in Malta. Historians have suggested that the basis for this similarity is that the people of the Apsheron peninsula were once connected to a seafaring Neolithic culture that flourished in the Mediterranean. This connection may have been forged by the rising sea levels following the most recent ice age 15,000 years ago. As polar caps thawed, water melted and drained southward through the Danube and Volga Rivers, causing the Black and Caspian Seas to rise. A cataclysmic flood followed between 12,000 and 11,000 BC. By 10,000 to 8000 BC, the Black and Caspian Seas may have joined, providing a sea link for explorers from the Mediterranean region. This connection may have allowed for the mixing of architectural styles, such as stone circles, throughout the Caucasus.

Some of Azerbaijan's most famous discoveries are the prehistoric petroglyphs of Gobustan, which were discovered just southwest of Baku. In 1939, Azerbaijani archaeologist Isaak Jafarzade began a scientific investigation that documented more than 3,500 of these rock paintings. Dated between the twelfth and eighth centuries BC, the petroglyphs depict stick figures among goats, cattle, and deer and reveal details about Neolithic life. Flints, shells, beads, and tools were also found at the Gobustan site.

This Neolithic petroglyph depicts the capture of a deer. Thousands of similar rock paintings have been found in Azerbaijan's Gobustan region. This particular painting is located in present-day Ankara, Turkey.

During the time the petroglyphs were produced, favorable living conditions in Gobustan supported a thriving culture. Adequate rainfall coupled with a fertile river valley made it possible for survival. Today Gobustan is arid semidesert.

2 ANCIENT EMPIRES

During the first millennium BC, Azerbaijan lay at the crossroads of migrating tribes and became incorporated into a series of empires. An early kingdom called Manna was formed around the ninth century BC, located in what is now southern Azerbaijan. Its inhabitants built stone fortresses to defend their cities from outside attack.

During the seventh century BC, the Scythians invaded the area that later became Azerbaijan. The Scythians were a seminomadic pastoral people who originated in central Asia. Their lifestyle required vast open spaces to graze their herds of domesticated animals. They rode horseback to cover the expansive terrain of the central Asian steppe, and they lived in portable felt tents. The Scythians survived by hunting and fishing; they also consumed mare's milk and

Danube River

GREECE
Athens O

Mediterranean Sea

EGYPT

This map shows the approximate migration route of the Scythians between the seventh and fifth centuries BC, a period in which Scythian nomads traveled west into the Caucasus region. Even though the Scythians were a highly developed tribal culture made up of warriors, priests, shepherds, and artisans, they had no written language. The Scythians crafted beautiful objects made from gold, used wheeled carts for transport, and drank fermented mare's milk, called *koumiss*.

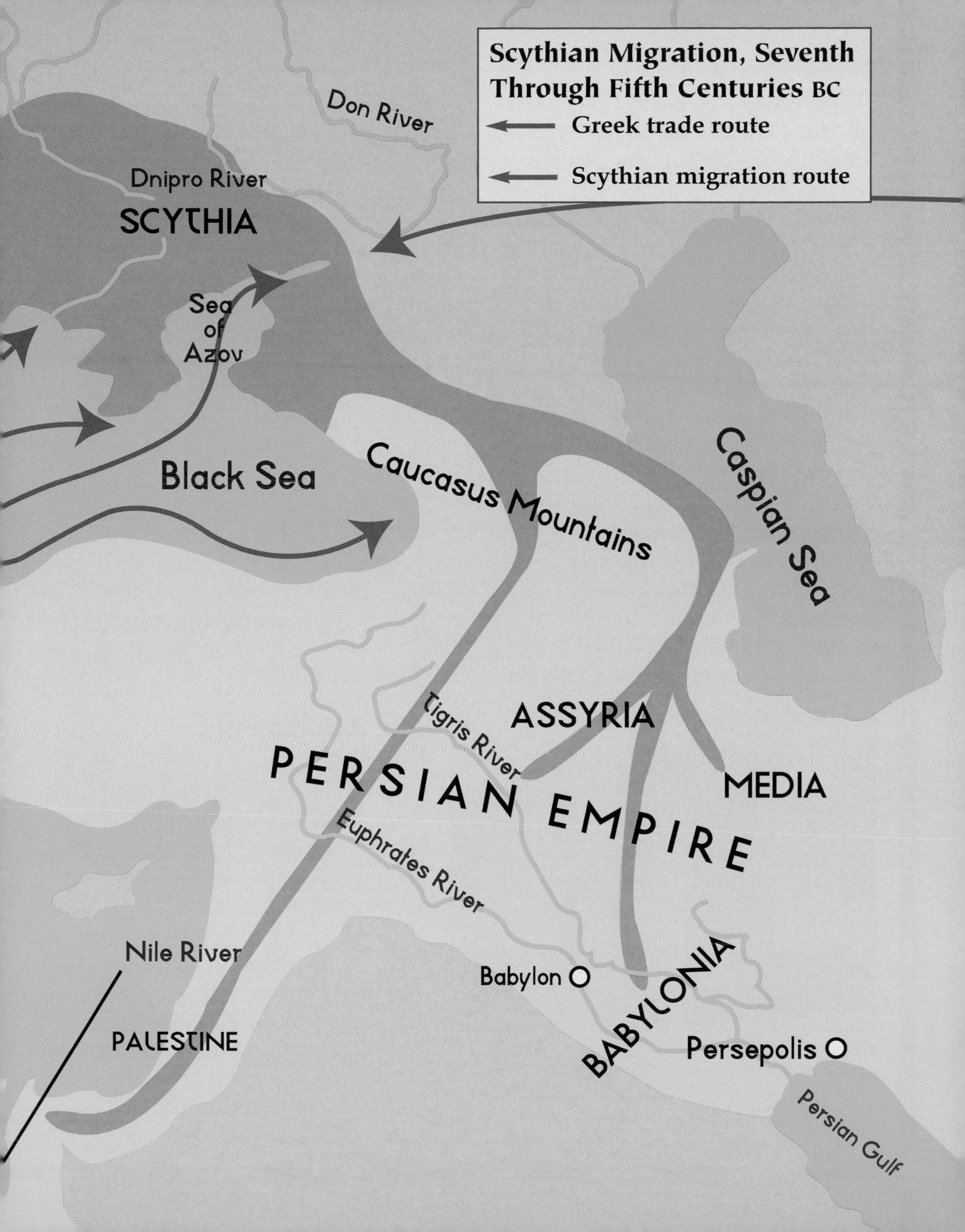
Scythian Migration, Seventh Through Fifth Centuries BC
Greek trade route
Scythian migration route
Don River
Dnipro River
SCYTHIA
Sea of Azov
Black Sea
Caucasus Mountains
Caspian Sea
ASSYRIA
Tigris River
PERSIAN EMPIRE
MEDIA
Euphrates River
Nile River
Babylon
BABYLONIA
PALESTINE
Persepolis
Persian Gulf

cheese. They eventually settled for longer periods once they cultivated wheat. At the height of their power, the Scythians occupied territories from the Don River in southern Russia to the Carpathian Mountains in central Europe.

The Scythians were succeeded by the Medes, an Aryan tribe from Persia (Iran). From the end of the seventh century to the early sixth century BC, the Medes dominated the region. The Manna kingdom fell and was absorbed by the Median Empire.

The Medes practiced the ancient religion of Zoroastrianism. The Zoroastrian prophet Zoroaster was born in Persia (present-day Azerbaijan) during the seventh century BC. He established Zoroastrianism, a monotheistic religion based on a cosmic battle between a supreme god of wisdom named Ahura Mazda and the struggle between good and evil forces represented by Ahura Mazda's sons, Spenta Mainyu (good) and Angra Mainyu (evil). Zoroastrians worshiped fire because they believed it represented the Holy Spirit of Ahura Mazda.

The Medes planned ring-shaped cities that surrounded a hilltop, where their local rulers lived in gold-painted palaces. Median ingenuity in fortress design deterred some of the strongest armies of the time, such as the Assyrians. An alliance made between the Babylonians and the Medes led to the destruction of the Assyrian capital of Nineveh in 612 BC.

Located just northeast of Baku in Surakhany, Azerbaijan, this sixth-century Zoroastrian temple was built over a pocket of natural gas that provided a constant flame for early Zoroastrian worshippers.

The Achaemenid Empire

Around 550 BC, the last Median king, named Astyages, was ousted. Astyages was imprisoned by his grandson Cyrus II, also known as Cyrus the Great, of Persia. Cyrus integrated the area of southern Azerbaijan into the Persian Achaemenid Empire, uniting the peoples of Persia. He went on to conquer territory that included the Middle East, central Asia, and

Persian artisans crafted this gold winged lion rhyton, an ancient animal-shaped drinking vessel, during the fifth century. Royalty of the Achaemenid Empire likely used the drinking cup for ceremonial purposes.

sections of south Asia, such as present-day Pakistan.

Cyrus was considered a liberator of the Jews. He freed them from slavery when he defeated the Babylonians in 539 BC and financed the rebuilding of their temple in Jerusalem. As a Zoroastrian, Cyrus sympathized with the Jews' monotheistic religious beliefs. Upon the conquest of Babylon, Cyrus issued a decree stating his policies in what is recognized to be the world's first declaration of human rights. It was inscribed on a clay cylinder and now resides in the British Museum in London.

King Darius I is credited with designing an efficient administration for the Achaemenid Empire. He developed an excellent communication system based on horse transport. Darius also created a centralized political system by dividing the empire into twenty *satrapies* (provinces) ruled by *satraps*, or local governors. To control the satraps, who may have, at times, aspired to greater power, each was paired

with a military commander loyal only to the king.

Zoroastrianism was the official religion of the Achaemenid Empire, but Darius allowed moderate religious freedom in the satrapies. As a devoted patron of the arts, Darius borrowed artistic styles from the Greeks to decorate his palace in the Persian capital of Persepolis. The influence of Greek culture on other civilizations is called Hellenism.

Alexander the Great

Eventually, the Achaemenid Empire began to weaken from within. Rebellions by Egyptians, Athenians, and Scythians weakened Persian dominance. The empire finally disintegrated due to a crushing blow dealt by Alexander the Great, king of Macedonia. Alexander cleverly defeated the armies of King Darius III in 331 BC, who had more than twice the number of troops, at the Battle of Gaugamela. He went on to invade the territories known later as Azerbaijan en route to capturing Persepolis. Alexander the Great created the largest empire the world had yet seen.

Around 328 BC, the Persian satrap of Media, Atropates, then serving Alexander the Great, formed an independent state called Atropatena along the Araks River, now in present-day Azerbaijan. Under his command,

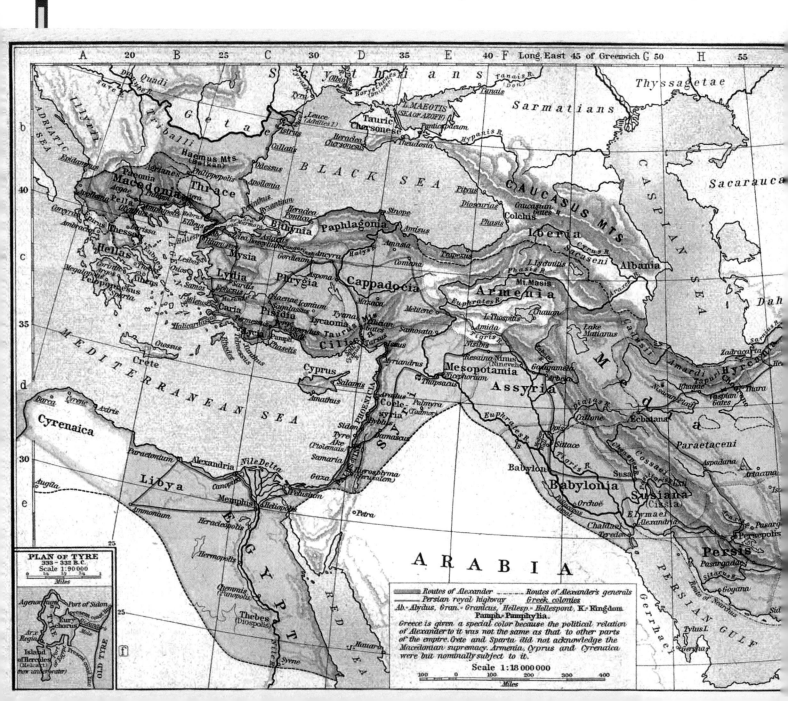

Atropates kept the land free from invaders and protected the freedom of the people living in this region.

The name "Azerbaijan" is often attributed to the Persian word for fire, *azar*, possibly because of the popularity of Zoroastrianism in the region; Zoroastrian temples were fueled by the region's rich oil deposits. During this time, Zoroastrianism dominated Atropatena. The capital of Atropatena, Gazaka, became a religious center.

Alexander the Great also acquired territory in northern Azerbaijan, which he called Caucasian Albania. This area was the land west of the Caspian Sea, between the Araks and Kura Rivers. Caucasian Albania was considered strategically important. It was a gateway to the Caucasus Mountains and a land bridge between Europe and Asia. Evidence in this link is revealed in Hellenistic coins that were minted and distributed in Caucasia, Albania, during this period. It was relatively independent from the Greek Macedonian rulers and remained so until the later Arab invasions of the seventh century AD.

While Alexander the Great had a reputation for being a ruthless general, he made important contributions to his empire, which included Egypt, Asia Minor (present-day Turkey), and parts of India. Taught by Aristotle as a boy, Alexander had great respect for classical learning and later founded the

This historical map illustrates the Macedonian Empire from 336 to 323 BC as well as the route Alexander and his armies took across central Asia. Although Alexander never crossed the lands later known as Azerbaijan, he appointed Atropates, satrap of Media, to rule over the territory. At the time, the southern portion of ancient Azerbaijan was known as Atropatena. This map was originally printed in a 1923 atlas.

Royal Library of Alexandria in Egypt. He championed the virtues of Hellenism, such as love of life; the celebration of drama, poetry, and wine; and worship of the Greek gods. Alexander had great respect for women, cherished his mother, Olympus, and advocated the fair treatment of women by his troops. Hellenistic styles influenced local art and architecture throughout his empire. Alexander also popularized the city-state model of government, which remains in place in parts of the Middle East and Asia.

Alexander also demanded that his troops worship him as they would a god, which eventually created great resentment. When several soldiers witnessed Alexander murder his friend, Clitus, they

This fifteenth-century Italian manuscript depicts Alexander the Great as a youth when he was a student of Aristotle's. The second-century Greek philosopher Aristotle taught Alexander for eight years.

became discouraged. Alexander's conquests ended in India, when his men refused to fight any longer. At thirty-three years of age, Alexander died in 323 BC.

After his death, the Macedonian Empire fragmented. It was torn apart by internal fighting among his successors, called the Diadochi. Caucasian Albania remained independent, but Atropatena was absorbed into a province controlled by the Macedonian general Seleucus. He founded the Seleucid dynasty in 312 BC, which ruled a vast territory that spanned from the Aegean Sea to central Asia. It included present-day Iran, Syria, Iraq, Azerbaijan, Lebanon, Afghanistan, and a large part of central Asia. In the second century BC, the Seleucid dynasty faced attacks by the Parthians along the Caspian Sea. The Parthians considered themselves heirs to the Achaemenid Empire and officially ended Macedonian dominance in Persia.

Roman Invasions

In 88 BC, the Parthian Empire was attacked by neighboring Armenia under Tigran the Great. (The current dispute between Armenia and Azerbaijan over the Nagorno-Karabakh region, discussed later in this book, can be traced back to this invasion.)

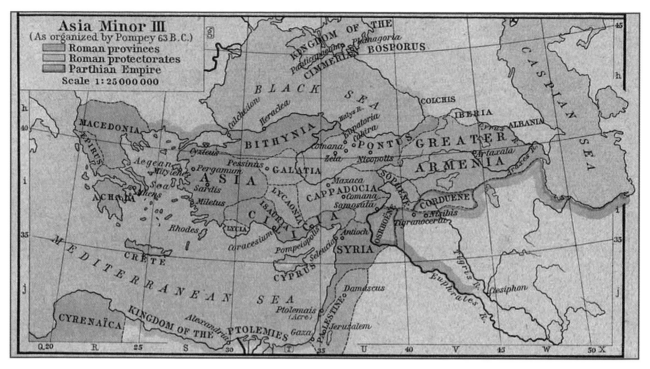

Campaigns by the Romans into Asia Minor (present-day Turkey) in 63 BC led by General Pompey are depicted in this historical map. Known as Pompey the Great after having led earlier battles for the Romans in both Spain and Africa, Pompey also rid the Mediterranean of pirates encroaching upon Roman trade ships. In 66 BC, Pompey had conquered Armenia, Syria, and Palestine, beginning the organization of the Eastern Roman Empire. Six years later, Pompey served with Caesar and Crassus in the First Triumvirate, a Roman political alliance.

The lands of both the Parthians and the Armenians were occupied in 66 BC by the Roman general Pompey, who took control of the Caucasus region. The Romans and Parthians battled on and off for nearly three centuries. During this time, Romans left graffiti, such as this message written in a cave in Gobustan: "Livius Julius Maximus, centurion of the XII Legion, came with the speed of heaven."

At its height, the Roman Empire controlled most of present-day Europe, the Balkans, North Africa, the Middle East, Turkey, and Caucasia. In doing so, the Romans laid the foundations of Western civilization.

The Romans introduced the idea of a centralized federal government, built a massive system of roads and aqueducts, and created the Julian calendar. Their contributions are still felt today. Although they were powerful and mighty, the Romans did not rule easily in the parts of their empire formerly dominated by Persia. The Romans replaced the Greeks as the Western enemy in the eyes of the Persians. As a result, they faced nearly constant warfare with the Persians for centuries.

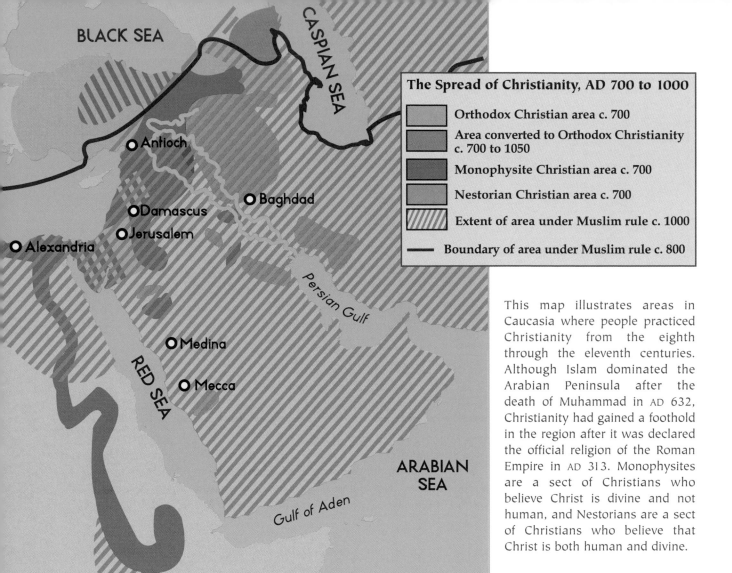

BLACK SEA

CASPIAN SEA

O Antioch

O Baghdad

O Damascus

O Jerusalem

O Alexandria

Persian Gulf

O Medina

RED SEA

O Mecca

Gulf of Aden

ARABIAN
SEA

The Spread of Christianity, AD 700 to 1000

Orthodox Christian area c. 700

Area converted to Orthodox Christianity c. 700 to 1050

Monophysite Christian area c. 700

Nestorian Christian area c. 700

Extent of area under Muslim rule c. 1000

Boundary of area under Muslim rule c. 800

This map illustrates areas in Caucasia where people practiced Christianity from the eighth through the eleventh centuries. Although Islam dominated the Arabian Peninsula after the death of Muhammad in AD 632, Christianity had gained a foothold in the region after it was declared the official religion of the Roman Empire in AD 313. Monophysites are a sect of Christians who believe Christ is divine and not human, and Nestorians are a sect of Christians who believe that Christ is both human and divine.

The Sassanid Dynasty

In AD 115, Romans withdrew from Caucasian Albania due to an epidemic of plague. The Parthians gained power again briefly but were defeated in 226 by another Persian dynasty called the Sassanids. The Sassanids believed the Parthians' customs had become too Hellenistic, and they wished to restore Persian culture to their empire. They also plotted to reclaim the territory of the Persian Achaemenid Empire, including Egypt, Syria, and Anatolia. The Sassanids frequently invaded Roman lands.

Christianity arrived in Caucasian Albania in the first century AD with the mission of St. Eliseus in Azerbaijan. By 313, the Albanian Church became a state institution, but early Christian converts were a minority group in Albania, as Zoroastrianism was preferred over

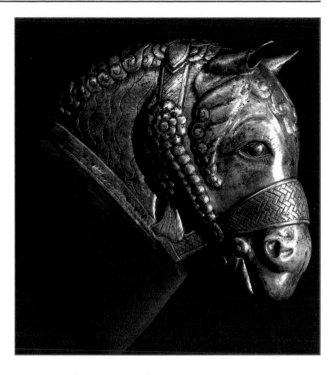

Sassanid artisans crafted beautiful gold artifacts like this fourth-century horse's head. Sassanid rulers wanted to restore the past culture and Zoroastrian religion of the Achaemenid Persians rather than welcome later Hellenistic traditions or Christianity.

other religions by its Sassanid rulers. The first Sassanid king, Ardashir I, accomplished a revival of Zoroastrianism by publishing holy texts in 226 called the *Zend Avesta*, which outlined the tenets of the religion.

In the fourth century AD, Constantine adopted Christianity as the official religion of the Byzantine Empire. The Sassanids battled fiercely in Byzantium, claiming Armenia in the process. As a result of the conflict, Sassanid Christians were now seen as an internal threat. Tolerance of Christianity in Caucasian Albania during this era decreased, and religious freedom depended on the whim of each ruler. In 409, during the reign of King Yazdigird III, also known as Yazdigird the Wicked, Christians were permitted to worship in public and build churches. Unfortunately, he changed his mind in 416, at which time Christians could no longer practice their religion. It wasn't until about seventy years later that Christianity was again tolerated.

At the end of the fifth century, the Sassanids faced attacks from the White Huns, nomads from central Asia. Sassanid king Khosrau I managed to control them, with the help of a new Turkic kingdom. Khosrau I also reclaimed Syria for the Sassanids, with a later successor, King Khosrau II, conquering Egypt.

The Sassanid dynasty came to end with King Yazdigird III, who was driven from his throne by the Arab caliphate in 641 and later murdered. The cumulative effects of a rigid social structure, years of warfare, and economic decline left the Sassanids weak and unable to resist the Arab invasion.

3 THE BIRTH OF ISLAM

BLACK SEA

Alexandria

Nile River

EGYPT

The Arabs took control of Caucasian Albania and Atropatena in 642, destroying both Christian churches and Zoroastrian temples in their wake. Arabs were devout followers of Islam and brought the new religion to the populations of both provinces, uniting the faithful. Zoroastrians in Azerbaijan and Persia fled to India and called themselves Parsis, another word for Persians. Today, India still hosts the world's largest remaining community of Parsis.

The Arabs dominated the territory of Azerbaijan, which they called Arran, from the seventh through the eleventh centuries. It became part of the Arab caliphate, but Azerbaijanis were never ruled directly by Arabs. They left administrative control to local elite rulers, called khans, and Arran was divided into several khanates. During this time, one of Baku's most beautiful monuments was created, a minaret called the Qiz Qalasi, or Maiden's Tower.

Islam, the religion based on the revelations of the prophet Muhammad, reached Caucasian Albania during the seventh century AD, as shown on this map. The religion gained adherents for four centuries until invading Mongol forces overran its Arab leaders. Although not all Azerbaijanis converted to Islam (many continued to practice Zoroastrianism), any nonpracticing Azerbaijanis had to pay heavy taxes to Muslim leaders and did not have the same rights and privileges as Muslims enjoyed.

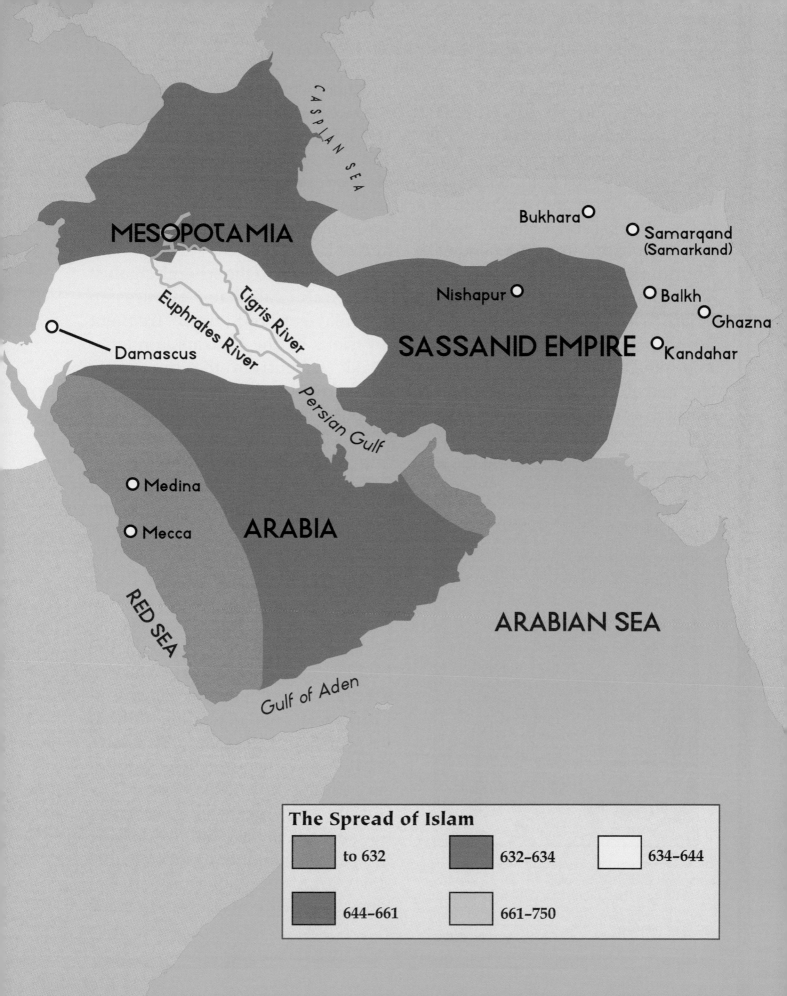

CASPIAN SEA

MESOPOTAMIA

Bukhara

Samarqand
(Samarkand)

Nishapur

Balkh

Ghazna

SASSANID EMPIRE

Kandahar

Tigris River

Euphrates River

Damascus

Persian Gulf

Medina

Mecca

ARABIA

RED SEA

ARABIAN SEA

Gulf of Aden

The Spread of Islam

to 632	632–634	634–644
644–661	661–750	

The Arab caliphate regularly extracted tribute (tax) money from the people of Arran and levied a hefty tax on those who did not convert to Islam. This eventually led to local uprisings. Throughout the eighth and ninth centuries, Azerbaijanis revolted against the caliphate for independence. Khurramites, a people who were descendants of Zoroastrians, led the largest of these rebellions. The Zoroastrian leader was named Babak Khorram-Din and was considered one of Azerbaijan's greatest heroes. He rebelled against Islam in Caucasian Albania between AD 816 and 837. Azerbaijani legend claims that Babak was betrayed by an Armenian leader and was executed. However, Babak's struggle succeeded in substantially weakening the caliphate's influence. Today his life story is a popular theme in Azerbaijani theater.

In addition to the struggle against the Arab caliphate, Caucasian Albania suffered from frequent invasions by the Khazars, a mighty Turkic tribe from the steppes of southern Russia. The occupying caliphate bore the brunt of Khazar attacks, decimating an entire Arab army in the Battle of Ardabil in 730. Seven years later, the Arab general Marwan forced the Khazar *khagan*, or supreme king, to convert to Islam and pledge allegiance to the caliphate. But by 861, Khagan Bulan converted again, this time to Judaism, and began a Jewish dynasty that lasted through the Middle Ages. He founded Khazaria, a region straddling the Black and Caspian Seas and extending north to present-day Ukraine. Khazaria became a center of religious tolerance during the Middle Ages.

With the caliphate now weakened, the latter half of the ninth century saw the rise of semi-independent feudal states in Arran. Albanian Christian kings assumed power again in some

The twelfth-century Qiz Qalasi, or Maiden's Tower, is a popular attraction in Baku. The nine-story tower, which harbors the remains of a well, was named after a woman who leapt from its top to avoid a pre-arranged marriage.

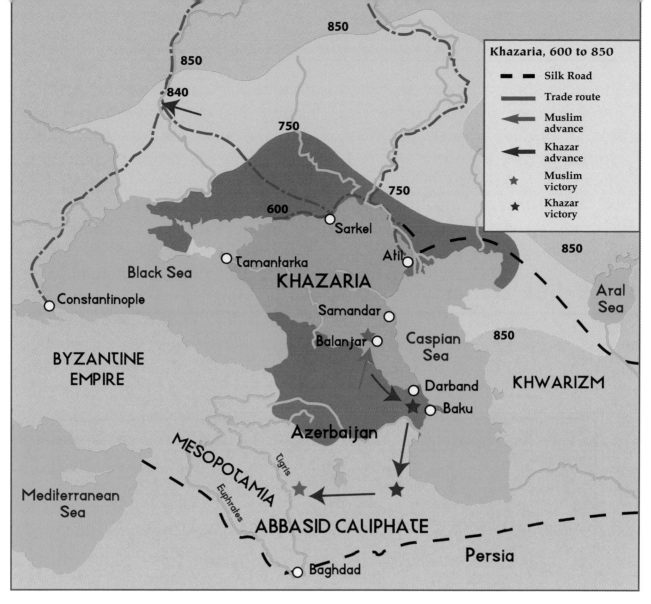

This map illustrates medieval Khazaria, a dynasty that developed in the northern Caucasus region between the Black and Caspian Seas during the seventh century AD. The Khazars were originally a nomadic Turkic people who originated in central Asia. Khazaria separated Christian and Muslim lands. Through a series of conflicts, its leaders prevented Islam from spreading north of the Caucasus Mountains. Even though Khazaria was the only place in the entire medieval world that expressed tolerance for all faiths, including both Christianity and Islam, its leaders adopted Judaism as their chosen religion.

cities, but many were ruled by Muslim dynasties. The most powerful was the Shirvan state, based in Shemaka in eastern Arran. The Shirvan Shah dynasty retained its independence from foreign rule until 1538 and became important to medieval Azerbaijan. Other memo-rable feudal lords of this period included the Ravvadids, who ruled from Tabriz in the south, and the Kurdish Shaddadids, with a capital in Ganja in the west.

During this time of relative peace, Azerbaijani cities such as Shaki, Shemakha, Baku, Tabriz, and

Kuba flourished. They were noted for the art they produced, such as works in ceramic, metal, and fiber, including carpet weaving and sericulture (silk making). This strengthened Azerbaijan's trade links with the other states in Caucasia and with Russia.

The Seljuk Dynasty

During the ninth and tenth centuries, a Turkic dynasty called the House of Seljuk began a series of conquests from its base north of the Aral Sea against rival tribes in western Asia. In 1018, the Seljuk warlord Tughril Beg, along with his brother Chagri Beg, reached Azerbaijan and defeated the Gaznavid dynasty. Mass migrations of Turkic tribes into Azerbaijan soon followed. The Seljuks pressed farther west and occupied Anatolia, effectively ending European domination of the area now known as Turkey. The Seljuks went on to rule the lands of Persia (Iran), Iraq, and Syria. They

I The Byzantine Empire in 1265.

Byzantine Empire
Greek Empire of Trebizond
Greek Despotat of Epirus
Kingdom of Bulgaria
Kingdom of Servia
Wallachian States
States under Latin rule
Palatinate of Cephalonia
Venetian possessions
Mongol dominions and Seljuk Turks
Dominion of the Mamelukes
Byz.Prov.-Byzantine Province
D.-Duchy, P-Principality
Scale 1:15 000 000

Territory ruled by the Turkic dynasty known as the House of Seljuk is illustrated in this historic map of the Roman Byzantine Empire during the thirteenth century. The Seljuks were warriors from central Asia who came to power beginning in the ninth century and who adopted Sunni Islam and defended the faith from Christian Crusaders.

Nizami Ganjavi

The Seljuk period contributed greatly to world literature, including the works of poet Nizami Ganjavi, who is hailed as a literary genius. He was born in AD 1141 in Ganja, then considered a cultural center of Azerbaijan. A well-educated man, Nizami wrote in Persian, then considered the scholarly language in medieval Asia. He is most famous for his five epic poems, later combined into a collection called Khamsa. Virtue, humanism, and the struggle for man to find his destiny are common themes. His lyrical writing style was infused with passionate emotion, and many of his poems were dedicated to his wife, Afaq (literally "Snow White" in Azerbaijani-Turkish). Nizami is noted for his adaptation of the romantic legend Leyli and Mejnun, a Muslim love story comparable to Shakespeare's *Romeo and Juliet*.

belonged to a Turkic tribe called the Oghuz, who played a key role in defending the Islamic faith against Christian crusaders. The Seljuks eventually brought an end to the Byzantine Empire. They were Sunni Muslims, a division or sect of Islam that believes the head of the Muslim community should be elected by the people.

The Seljuks had a profound impact on the character and culture of Azerbaijan, and by the fourteenth century, its people were essentially a mixture of Turkic and Persian ancestry. Azerbaijanis adopted the Seljuks' Turkic language and blended it with Persian words, which later evolved into the modern Azerbaijani tongue.

The Seljuk dynasty divided into several independent kingdoms by 1127, under separate leaders known as *alabegs* or *atabeks*. In 1136, the Seljuk Shams ad-din Ildeniz created a minor Seljuk kingdom in Azerbaijan. This kingdom thrived in the twelfth century, bringing forth a Muslim renaissance that advanced the arts and sciences.

Nakhichevan, a territory of Azerbaijan that now lies in Armenia, became the capital of the Atabek kingdom of Ilgizids in the twelfth century. Significant advances in mathematics were made during this period.

Many architectural masterpieces were also created during this period, one of the most notable being the mausoleum of Momine-khatun, the wife of Ildegizid Atabek Djakhan Pakhlevan. The architect, Ajami Nakhchivani, built this massive tomb in 1186, the largest and finest in Azerbaijan. It was essentially a brick tower, but the application of a turquoise blue glaze turned it into a stunning sight. Ornamentation such as rosettes, octahedrons, and five-pointed stars made for a dazzling display of geometry.

4 MEDIEVAL EMPIRES

As the Seljuks focused on expanding their empire westward into Turkey, they left Caucasia unprotected and vulnerable to attack. The cultural renaissance in Azerbaijan came to an abrupt halt in the thirteenth century during the violent invasions of Mongol horsemen from central Asia. The first round of Mongol attacks was led by Genghis Khan, called "the Scourge of God" by the Muslims he conquered. After seizing China, Genghis Khan ravaged his way through Caucasia and southern Russia, leaving a bloodbath in his wake and looting the kingdoms of any wealth. Genghis Khan's grandson Hülegü Khan, who conquered Azerbaijan and Persia in 1256, dealt the final blow. The Mongols set up a regional capital in Tabriz, now a part of Iran, which became a major commercial and political hub of the Mongol

MEDITERRANEAN SEA

RED SEA ———

Genghis Khan (right), shown in an eighteenth-century portrait by Pierre Duflos, was the founder of the Mongol Empire. Genghis Khan, a title that can be translated as "prince of all that lies between the oceans," was a superior military ruler who had been trained to fight since childhood. Between the years 1220 and 1222, Genghis Khan conquered one city after another, including Bukhara, Samarqand, Herat, Nishapur, and Merv. After his death in 1227, his empire was divided between two of his sons, Ögödei and Chagatai, who continued to expand Mongol dominions.

EUROPE

Caspian Sea

Aral Sea

Bukhara
(Bukhoro)

○ **Samarqand**
(Samarkand)

Merv ○

○ **Herat**

Nishapur

ARABIAN SEA

Karakorum
(Captial of Mongol
Empire after 1235) ○

MONGOLIA

Gobi Desert

CHINA

GENGISKAN,
Grand Mogol.

Mongol Empire

 Mongols 1227

Mongols 1280

Empire. The Mongols crushed Baghdad in 1258 and officially ended the Abbasid caliphate. The new Mongol rulers called themselves the il-Khans, or viceroys. The Mongols practiced shamanism, a religion based on the belief of an unseen world that is only accessible to the person known as the shaman.

The il-Khans extracted a heavy tax from their subjects, particularly for east-west trade. The upshot of this was increased protection along trade routes, as no one wished to make trouble with the Mongols. They were the first to print paper money in the West, a place where coins were the only currency. The Mongols were able to rule their territory as a unified state until 1335, when it fractured into rival provinces. At its height, the Mongol Empire stretched from present-day Korea in the east to as far as Germany in the west.

The Mongols destroyed much of what the Seljuks had built in Azerbaijan and largely murdered or

A Persian artist created this fifteenth-century painting of two warriors fighting. The Mongols were fierce and disciplined soldiers who lived according to Genghis Khan's laws. Organized Mongol armies, which emerged under the leadership of Genghis Khan in 1206, traveled on horseback in columns and within riding distance of Mongol messengers, who would communicate with soldiers and help control invasions.

enslaved its people. It was a dark time in the country's history, and the region served as a battleground for invasions from a rival Mongol tribe called the Golden Horde. The infamous Mongol emperor, Timur the Great, ruled an empire from Iraq to India. Unfortunately for the Azerbaijanis, Timur chose to wage war against the Golden Horde within the borders of Azerbaijan. Only after Timur's disappearance between 1403 and 1405 did the Mongol Empire crumble. This decline of Mongol dominance revived the old principalities of Azerbaijan, most notably the dynasty of the Shirvan Shahs.

Tribal Dominance

As the Mongols lost their grasp on their empire, the Turkmen, a people related to the same Turkic tribes of the Seljuks, dominated Azerbaijan for about a century. Two of the most powerful Turkic confederations were the rival clans the Qara-Qoyunlu, or Black Sheep, and the Aq-Qoyunlu, or White Sheep.

The Qara-Qoyunlu took control of present-day Azerbaijan, Armenia, and Iraq in 1410, and reached their peak of power under Sultan Jahanshah. He ruled from the former Mongol capital of Tabriz until his death in 1467 at the hands of the Aq-Qoyunlu clan. They sacked Tabriz and murdered Jahanshah under the leadership of Uzun Hasan, taking the Qara-Qoyunlu territories. The Aq-Qoyunlu suffered invasions from their neighboring despots, the Timurids. Even though the Timurids were ancestors of Timur, they captured the Timurid leader Abu Sa'id and killed him. Through future battles, the Aq-Qoyunlu clan extended its territory to include present-day Georgia, western Turkey, and parts of Iran.

At the same time as the clashes among the Turkic clans was a flourishing of the Shirvan Shah dynasty once again. The Shirvan Shahs of Azerbaijan gave the invaders their allegiance. They accepted the

The Blue Mosque in Tabriz, Iran, a former capital of the Mongol Empire, was built in 1465 under the leadership of the Turkic leader Sultan Jahanshah. Shortly after its completion, it was severely damaged in 1467 during raids by Turkmen known as the Black Sheep.

The Mongol Dominions, 1300—1405.

This historic map shows the extent of the Mongol Empire from 1300 to 1405. This century marks the leadership of Genghis Khan's sons Ögödei and Chagatai; his grandson Kublai Khan; and Timur the Great. It was during these successive reigns that the empire was broken into four distinct regions until the violent campaigns of Timur between 1336 and 1405. Timur, although he reportedly had a love of art and scholarship, is remembered most for his vicious and destructive warfare. Much of the Mongol Empire was again united for a period until Timur died in 1405 and his grandson was appointed successor in 1406.

domination of their foreign affairs by the Seljuks and Timurids. This arrangement allowed the wealthy Shirvans to live in peace and prosperity. The fifteenth century saw the creation of the splendid Shirvan Shah's palace in Baku, built by the last Shirvan, Kalil Allah I.

Around this time, a Persian dynasty called the Safavids began to mobilize support behind religious fervor. The Safavids were Shiite Muslims. Shiites believe that after the prophet Muhammad there will be no other prophets of Allah, their God. In addition, Shiites believe that the only true spiritual leader of man is the imam, who is directly appointed by Allah. Thus, matters of law and politics are also to be judged by the imam in Shiite practice. This had a profound impact on government matters, for in the more moderate Sunni sect, there is a separation between matters of religion and matters of state. The Safavids went on missions to spread their revolutionary message and were known as Qizilbash, or "redheads," after the red headgear they wore. The leader of the emerging Safavid Shiite movement was named Haydar, and he was married to the daughter of the Aq-Qoyunlu ruler, Uzun Hasan.

Haydar clashed with Uzun Hasan's successor and son, Ya'qub,

after Hasan's death in 1478. Ya'qub formed an alliance with the Shirvan Shahs and, sensing Haydar's growing influence, had Haydar killed. Haydar's son, Ismai'l, then went into exile in Anatolia, plotting to overthrow the Aq-Qoyunlu and establish a Shiite state. In 1501, he achieved his goal and defeated the Aq-Qoyunlu in battle in Azerbaijan. Tabriz was now the seat of the Safavid Shiite empire. Persian culture ascended in Azerbaijan. Azerbaijanis converted from Sunnism to Shiism, as they remain today.

The Safavid Dynasty

The Safavid dynasty reigned in Azerbaijan from 1501 until 1736. It ruled a territory that included Iran, Iraq, and eastern Anatolia, which bordered the powerful Ottoman Empire. While the Safavids expanded trade and brought prosperity for Azerbaijan, they constantly feuded with the Ottoman Turks for control over trade routes and differences between their Sunni and Shiite beliefs. Ottoman threats forced the Safavids to move their capital from Tabriz to Qazvin.

Azerbaijan was divided into several khanates, including Shirvan, Baku, Ganja, Karabakh, and Nakhichevan. The Safavids waged a holy war against Christian infidels in neighboring Georgia and were cruel to the Sunni Muslims they encountered. Much of the Safavids' energy went into warring with the Ottoman Turks to the northwest. The Safavids' resources were further taxed by battling with the Uzbeks to the east and the Portuguese in the Middle East. Despite this constant warfare, the Safavids created some of the most splendid works of architecture and art of this period.

The Ottoman Empire

The rival Ottomans originally came to power in the fourteenth century. The Ottomans were led by a Muslim Turk named Osman I, who conquered the weakened Byzantine

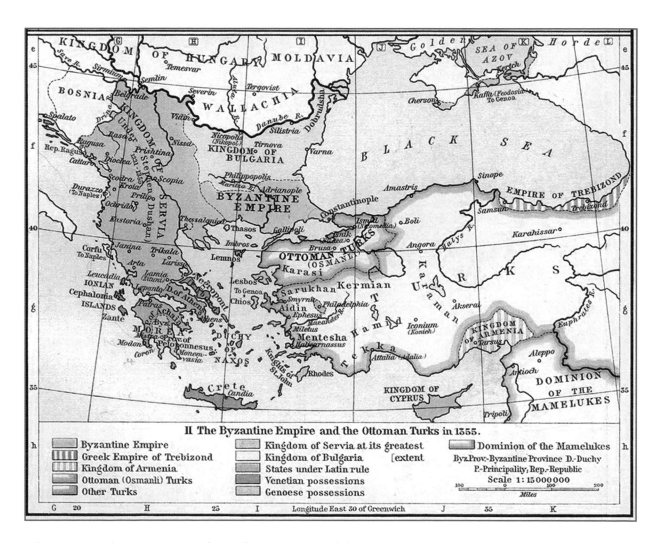

This nineteenth-century map shows the emergence of the Ottoman Empire and the extent to which it had expanded in 1355. The Ottoman Empire was founded by a group of Turkish nomads living in Asia Minor who were led by Osman I. Its core had first developed within the Christian Byzantine Empire, which had earlier been weakened by invading Mongol forces during the thirteenth century. Osman I died in 1326 and was given the title of *ghazi*, or holy Islamic warrior, after his death.

Empire. Thus began a reign that lasted nearly 700 years. At their height, the Ottomans occupied Asia Minor (Turkey), the Balkan Peninsula, islands in the eastern Mediterranean, Vienna, sections of Hungary, Poland, Russia, the Middle East, Arabia, and North

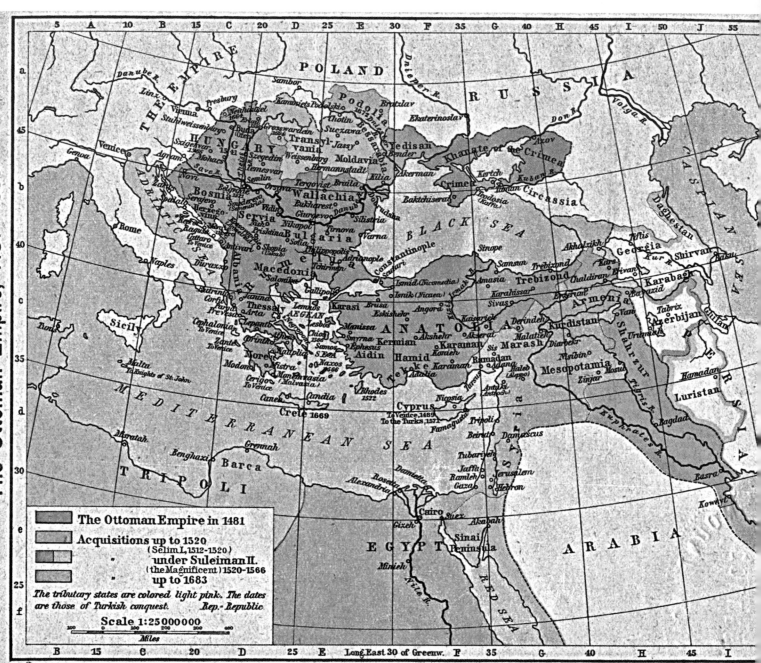

The Ottoman Empire, pictured in this nineteenth-century map, is shown at various stages of development between 1481 and 1683. The empire had reached its greatest expanse under Sultan Süleyman II the Magnificent, who reigned between 1520 and 1566. The Ottoman Empire had grown steadily since the death of Osman I in 1326, but it had made its greatest territorial gains during the sixteenth century.

Africa. The former Byzantine capital of Constantinople was then referred to by its Turkish name, Istanbul.

Not unlike the Safavids, the Ottomans wished to conquer the world for Islam, the difference being they favored the Sunni sect. To attain this goal, the Ottomans would often capture boys from invaded lands, forcibly convert them to Islam, and then use them for military service. As a result of the Ottoman invasions, Muslim cultural influence penetrated European territory. From their base in Turkey, the Ottomans crossed the Bosporous Sea and took present-day Bulgaria, Serbia, and Bosnia-Herzegovina, all the way south to Albania.

The Ottomans occupied eastern Caucasia from 1578 until 1603. Georgia became a divided land, controlled in the east by the Safavids and in the west by the Ottomans. The Safavids remained strong despite the constant feuds, and they flourished once again under Shah Abbas I, who ruled from 1578 until 1629. He removed the Ottoman Turks and regained Tabriz. Under Abbas prosperity returned to Persia. Shah Abbas created a strong infrastructure by building new roads and bridges, encouraged the silk trade with India, and cultivated relationships with Western nations. To ensure stability, he enforced strict adherence to Shiism. His successors were less influential leaders, however, and brutally fought among themselves. By the early eighteenth century, Safavid power weakened. Frequent warfare with the Ottomans, internal conflicts, and an Afghan invasion dismantled the dynasty. In 1726, the Ottomans had invaded Azerbaijan again.

A notorious warrior named Nadir Shah entered the scene in 1729, uniting the Aq-Qoyunlu and Qara-Qoyunlu clans against the Ottomans. Nadir Shah was a fierce fighter who led successful battles against the Afghans under the Safavid leader Shah Sultan Husayn. Nadir recaptured Tabriz in 1730 and continued to remove the Ottomans from Persia (Iran) and Azerbaijan. When the Safavids squandered his victory by reconciling with the Turks, Nadir Shah deposed the leadership of the current shah, an infant son named Abbas III, and seized power. Nadir Shah was declared king of Persia in 1736, effectively ending the Safavid dynasty. Eventually, all territory lost to the Ottomans was regained under Nadir Shah, and a third of Turkey itself was occupied by Persia. Nadir Shah attempted to unite Shiite Persia

Nadir Shah, who was king of Persia (Iran) in 1736, is pictured in this eighteenth-century engraving. Although his strong leadership helped Persia flourish during his reign, he ultimately became mentally ill. As a result of Nadir Shah's increasingly poor judgment and inability to lead Persia, he was murdered in 1747.

with the Sunni Ottoman Empire, but this angered the Shiite population, and the idea was abandoned. Nadir Shah's successes gained him Oman on the Arabian Peninsula and parts of Mughal India, including Delhi. It was in the city of Delhi where he had previously stolen the Koh-i-noor diamond and the Peacock Throne, gaining wealth for Persia. Under Nadir Shah, Persia's empire flourished. But while his power grew, Nadir Shah's mental faculties failed. He so feared opposition from his son that he had him blinded. His reign came to an end in 1747 when he was killed in a coup by one of his guards.

5 RUSSIAN IMPERIALISM

In the early eighteenth century, the Russian Empire began to take an interest in Caucasia, which profoundly affected Azerbaijan's history for the next 300 years. Persia and Turkey continued to fight over possession of trade routes in the region, but an expanding Russian Empire seized Baku in 1722 under Russian czar Peter the Great. Fearing a Turkish invasion of this Persian-controlled territory, Peter the Great led a successful campaign that opened the Caspian Sea for Russian commerce.

Peter the Great was impressed by both European military tactics and Europe's thriving cultural life. He utilized much of what he learned from a youthful voyage to Europe in order to improve the Russian navy, beautify Russia's cities, and introduce social reforms. St. Petersburg, a city in northwestern Russia named for the czar, became Russia's new capital. Peter the Great is credited with advancing Russia toward improvements in government, industry, technology, and art.

The Russian Empire continued to expand its authority in Caucasia throughout the nineteenth century. The Georgian king, Georgi XII, abdicated authority to Czar Paul I of Russia in exchange for protection in 1801. The Russians gradually overpowered Persia for political control over northern Azerbaijan. They took the cities of Baku, Sheki, Shemakha, Ganja, and Lenkoran, and

The Principality of Moscow about 1300
The Grand Principality of Moscow or Muscovy (Great Russia) in 1462
Boundary of the dominions of the Golden Horde (Khanate of Kipchak) till 1480
Routes of Tatar raids
Acquisitions under Ivan III. (1462-1505)
" " Vasili III. (1505-1533)
" " Ivan IV. (1533-1584, Tsar 1547)
" " Feodor and Boris Godunov (1584-1605)
" " Michael Romanov (1613-1645)
" " Alexis (1645-1676)
" " Peter the Great (1682-1725)
" " Anna (1730-1740)
" " Elizabeth (1741-1762)
" " Catherine II. (1762-1796)

Partitions of Poland
First partition, 1772.
To Russia
" Prussia
" Austria
Second partition, 1793.
To Russia
" Prussia
Third partition, 1795.
To Russia
" Prussia
" Austria

The region inclosed within the line
was held by Russia from
1723 to 1732 only. That bordered in
purple was not finally acquired until 1801; and that bordered in pink,
not until about 1865.
The names of the principal peoples
of Russia are printed in italics.
For the growth of Russia in Asia,
see p. 170/171

Scale 1:15 000 000
100   100   200
Miles

they profited from the control of their trade routes. While Persia retained control of Azerbaijan's southern territory, two treaties drawn after wars between Russia and Persia set Azerbaijan's present-day borders. The Treaty of Gulistan (1813) formed a Russo-Persian border along the Araks River, and the Treaty of Turkmanchay (1828) gained Russia the Nakhichevan khanates. The province of Nakhichevan lies within Armenian territory along the border with Turkey, a situation that led to brutal clashes between Azerbaijan and Armenia over the possession of Nakhichevan.

The Russians divided Azerbaijan into three administrative zones: Baku in the east, Elizavetpol in central Azerbaijan, and the Yerevan province in the west, which also included much of Armenia. Although the major decisions of Azerbaijani political life were being made thousands of miles away in St. Petersburg, Russian rule brought economic stability to Azerbaijan. The Russians controlled Christian Armenia as well and encouraged Armenians to immigrate to Azerbaijan. Many Armenians went as refugees from wars with Turkey and Persia, while others left with the hope of financial success. While the Armenians were skilled craftsmen, traders, and educators who made important contributions to nineteenth-century Azerbaijani society, the Azerbaijanis resented their presence. They felt that the Christian Armenians, many who expressed anti-Muslim sentiments, were favored by Russians since they held many administrative posts in the Russian monarchy.

Although the Russians dominated Azerbaijan's political and economic affairs in the nineteenth century, Persian and Turkish culture prevailed. Azerbaijanis remained devout Muslims. They did not adopt Christian Orthodoxy as practiced in Russia, Armenia, and Georgia. The Russians were mainly interested in extracting commodities from Azerbaijan, such as manganese ore, lumber, walnuts, tobacco, silk, wool, fruits, and animal hides. The Russians built railroads that linked Baku with Batumi on the Black Sea. They also constructed the Georgian Military Highway, which ran north-south across the Caucasus

This historical map illustrates the growth of the Russian Empire in Europe between 1300 and 1796. Azerbaijan was conquered and made part of Russia after a 1722 invasion led by Peter the Great (inset), who was a talented military leader and the Russian czar. Peter the Great is remembered most for aggressively modernizing seventeenth-century Russia, a place he believed was isolated and underdeveloped. As emperor of the Russian Empire, a title that he gave himself in 1721 and held until his death in 1725, he founded St. Petersburg, a city modeled after those in Europe.

The Wealth of Asia

Russia's interest in central Asia began after invasions under Ivan the Terrible in 1554, at which time a Mongol kingdom on the Volga River was conquered. Ivan's son, Fyodor, continued these incursions, and by the time Peter the Great set foot in Asia, it was clear that the potential to exploit its agricultural lands could boost the Russian economy. This idea of exploiting one country's resources in order to empower another country is known as imperialism.

This painting of Ivan the Terrible, the first czar of Russia from 1547 until 1584, was created by Viktor Mihajlovic Vasnetsov. Ivan waged a war to expand Russia for twenty-two years and laid the groundwork for its feudal economy.

Mountains, speeding up the transport of goods in the region.

Black Gold

Petroleum, much of it deposited in the Caspian Sea, became Azerbaijan's most valuable commodity. In 1848, the world's first industrial oil well was drilled on the Bibi-Heybat field in Azerbaijan, and by 1873, the first gusher flowed. At its height, this well produced 3,000 tons (2,722 metric tons) per day, which led to the development of large-scale oil production technology. Russians and Armenians immigrated to Azerbaijan to take advantage of the Baku oil boom, adding a diverse character to its capital city. The population of Baku expanded from 13,000 in 1860 to more than 112,000 by 1897, making it the largest city in Caucasia. Azerbaijanis played an active role in their economy, dominating the business of oil transport in the Caspian

Crude oil gushes from a well in Baku in this artist's rendering. Azerbaijan was a major oil-producing nation in the early twentieth century until the 1950s, when the Soviet Union redirected oil production elsewhere. Since the mid-1990s, offshore drilling of untapped oil resources in the Caspian Sea has increased its production.

in Azerbaijan, compared with 9 million tons (8,164,800 metric tons) in the United States. Azerbaijan was supplying 95 percent of Russia's oil needs and 50 percent of the world's. Within five years, nearly one-third of Baku's population were ethnic Russians, along with Armenians and Jews. Oil had attracted scores of immigrants to Baku, and they now dominated that city's population and politics. Three scripts were now commonplace in Azerbaijan: Cyrillic, Latin, and Arabic. Social unrest began to boil over as Azerbaijan thirsted for independence from Russian control.

Nationalist Strivings

The name of Azerbaijan's capi Baku, comes from the combination of Azeri words *bad* and *kube*, which literally means "buffeted b winds." The fierce winds of the Caspian Sea in Baku were similar to the storm of anger that was brewing in Azerbaijan at the turn of the twentieth century. Azerbaijanis began voicing their nationalist aspirations. Russia's main concern in Azerbaijan was to exploit oil reserves and to keep order, by force if necessary.

Sea. About 30 percent of the oil businesses were Azerbaijani-owned.

By 1901, 11 million tons (9,979,200 metric tons) of oil had been produced

The public's welfare was of little concern to authorities. The workers and upper classes agitated for political reform, but much of Azerbaijan was still populated by peasants. By

Baku, seen in this artist's rendering that depicts the city around 1885, has been the capital of Azerbaijan since 1920. Primarily a city known for its production of petroleum, Baku is a maze of both medieval and contemporary structures, including its original fortress, several mosques and palaces, and archaeological sites that prove it was once the site of an ancient settlement.

the early 1900s, the oil boom was ending, and Azerbaijan was gripped by an economic depression. Radical and reform parties began to organize. Violence broke out among Azerbaijanis and Armenians, both jockeying for local control.

Baku became an incubator for revolutionary forces, with its proletariat, or working class, toiling under Russian control. A group of Azerbaijani intellectuals formed a leftist (radical liberal) party called Himmat in 1903. It was a group of nationalists concerned with promoting Azerbaijani culture and language, which they feared would be consumed by Russian dominance. They also felt that oil revenues were only benefiting foreigners.

At the same time, the Russian and Armenian populations in Baku formed a Social Democratic Party, which paralleled the spirit of Communism that was developing in

Russia. Some members of Himmat, who were now starting to ally themselves with the Communists, broke off from the party. They formed the popular Musavat, or Equality Party, in 1912, which set its sights on an independent Azerbaijan. They gained mass appeal on a platform of progressive reforms and Azerbaijani nationalism.

World War I erupted in 1914, as a result of territorial and economic rivalry that had been brewing among the colonial superpowers, Germany, France, and Great Britain, since the latter half of the nineteenth century. World War I also involved the participation of many additional countries as a result of a complex web of alliances. Turkey sided with Germany and was a part of the Central powers, which also included the Austria-Hungarian Empire and Italy. Russia united with England and France's Allied powers, which the

United States ultimately supported. The war had a devastating effect on human lives and the economy. Brutal trench warfare killed millions and demoralized a generation. The Russians also suffered devastating losses during the conflict, which caused increased discontent at home.

While the Azerbaijanis saw the Russians as their oppressors, many Russians felt just as dissatisfied. Many were still landless peasants as they had been under the Czar with few freedoms, despite emancipation from serfdom in 1861. Russians continually paid heavy taxes to fund the empire's military. As a result, the czar lived a life of luxury while most people suffered. It was in this atmosphere that the Communist philosophy took hold, which promoted the liberation of the workers. A 1905 Communist coup initially failed, but the huge losses suffered during World War I were the final motivation to overthrow the czarist regime. Czar Nicholas II abdicated under the persuasion of his Russian Army of the High Command and fled to Siberia. He and his family were then executed on July 16, 1917.

By October 1917, the Bolsheviks, led by Vladimir Ilyich Lenin, seized control of St. Petersburg, which had been renamed Petrograd. The Bolsheviks adopted the slogan "Peace, bread, and land." Peasants could now own property. Russia soon became engulfed in a civil war between loyalists and the new Soviet rulers. This period of revolution and unrest set the stage for Azerbaijan to jockey for its own freedom from tyranny.

A Taste of Freedom

Drawing inspiration from recent events in Russia, the Baku

Vladimir Ilyich Lenin (1870–1924), disguised as a worker in this photograph taken during the Russian Revolution, was a lawyer and Communist theorist. Lenin led the Bolsheviks to overthrow the Russian government in 1917, along with Leon Trotsky, Aleksey Rykov, and Joseph Stalin, who became the Soviet dictator in 1926.

The children seen marching in this 1917 photograph taken during the Russian Revolution were demanding an eight-hour workday. Poor treatment and wages, long hours, and unsafe working conditions caused Russian textile workers to strike, demanding a Socialist Russian state.

The Musavat Party dominated the new Azerbaijani government based in Baku. Although Azerbaijan was technically an independent nation, it remained occupied by Turkish troops until the end of World War I in 1918. The Allies defeated the Central powers, and the Turks were replaced by British troops in Azerbaijan.

Fearing invasion because of the growing ambitions of the Red Army, Azerbaijan tried to unite with Persia, but its brief independence came to an end. The Red Army occupied Azerbaijan with little resistance in April 1920. At the time of the occupation, Azerbaijanis were preoccupied, fighting a separatist movement by Armenians in south-central Azerbaijan. In September 1920, Azerbaijan signed a treaty uniting its economy, military, and foreign trade with Soviet Russia. Lenin justified the invasion in the name of Caspian oil reserves to service the Bolshevik cause. This occupation turned into seventy-one years of total political and economic control by the Soviet Union.

Bolsheviks—composed mainly of Russians and Armenians—declared a Marxist state in Azerbaijan. Muslim nationalists calling themselves the Army of Islam, with heavy military support provided by Ottoman Turks, marched on Baku and defeated the Bolsheviks. They established the Azerbaijan People's Democratic Republic in May 1918, and Azerbaijan became an independent Muslim nation. The Armenian population living in Baku suffered a violent backlash.

6

THE
SOVIET ERA

In 1922, the newly named Union of Soviet Socialist Republics (USSR) forged a single state composed of Azerbaijan, Armenia, and Georgia called the Transcaucasian Federated Soviet Socialist Republic (SFSR). All three states withdrew their rights to determine policies to the authority of the SFSR.

The Red Army also invaded Nakhichevan, an Azerbaijani enclave located near the borders of Armenia, Turkey, and northern Iran. Since Nakhichevan's population largely wanted to be bound to Azerbaijan, two treaties signed by Russia, Turkey, and Transcaucasia officially linked the territories. In 1924, Nakhichevan became an independent republic of Azerbaijan, which it remains today. The strategic location of a Soviet presence along the border with Iran gave the Russians an excuse to further expand.

The Stalin Era

Joseph V. Stalin succeeded Lenin as head of the Soviet Union in 1926 and embarked on a dictatorship that lasted until 1953. Stalin dismembered the SFSR in 1936, and Azerbaijan became a separate republic of the Soviet Union. With its capital at Moscow, the USSR controlled Azerbaijan's political, economic, and social policies. It took over all of Azerbaijan's industries, including its prized oil business. Local

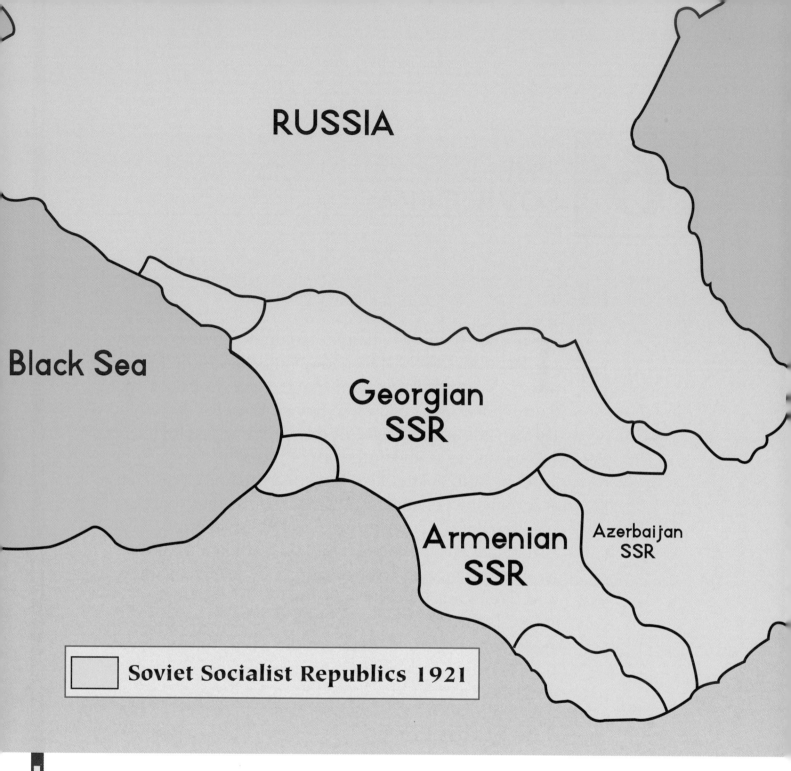

RUSSIA

Black Sea

Georgian SSR

Armenian SSR

Azerbaijan SSR

Soviet Socialist Republics 1921

Azerbaijan, seen in this map of Soviet Socialist Republics in 1921, was then a part of a single Soviet state composed of Azerbaijan, Armenia, and Georgia. Following a short three-month period of independence, invading Soviet Red Army soldiers forced Azerbaijan into the Transcaucasian Federated Soviet Socialist Republic (SFSR) in 1922. Fourteen years later, in 1936, Azerbaijan became a republic of the Union of Soviet Socialist Republics (USSR), a status it held until its independence in 1991.

Caspian Sea

enterprise diminished as thousands of people migrated to the larger cities of Baku and Sumgait to work in Soviet refineries and factories.

The Stalin era was characterized by a drive to establish state-owned, centrally controlled industry and agriculture ruled with an iron fist that often stamped out human rights. Stalin created the collective farm program, which forced farmers to grow mass supplies of cash crops, such as cotton, for Soviet textile mills. In the past, local farms grew crops for the local market, but the mass collectivization of farms was meant to serve the larger Soviet machinery. Azerbaijani farmers who protested these policies were sent to work camps, imprisoned in Siberia, or killed. Writers, scientists, and other intellectuals were often treated brutally during the Stalinist regime. These programs also left huge environmental scars in the region. While Stalinism brought cruel oppression to the people of Azerbaijan, it can also be said that significant gains in industry and literacy were achieved during this time, especially compared with achievements in other Muslim countries during the same period.

World War II broke out in Europe in 1939, and the Soviet Union fought with the Allied forces. The Soviet Union suffered much destruction along its western borders during the conflict, and many Azerbaijanis lost their lives. During this time, the Soviet Union used the war as an excuse to expand its territory into Iran. The Red Army, now with a strong foothold in southern Caucasia, occupied northern Iran in 1941, under the guise of uniting the Azerbaijani populations of both countries. The Soviets encouraged separatists in Iranian Azerbaijan. They called on the Democratic Party of Azerbaijan to rebel against the Iranian government. In 1945, the Autonomous Government of Azerbaijan, actually a Soviet satellite state, was formed in Tabriz. This lasted only briefly, as Western forces insisted that the Soviet Union should return the territory to Iran in 1946. The separatist rebellion encouraged by the Red Army resulted in a backlash of abuse against Azerbaijanis in Iran and a suppression of their culture. As a result, contact among Azerbaijanis living along the

Joseph Stalin *(left)* is seen walking with the Soviet military leader and Bolshevik party member Kliment Yefremovich Voroshilov in this undated painting. Voroshilov was a prominent politician closely associated with Stalin, who led the Red Army during the Russian Civil War (1918–1920). Voroshilov was elected by the Communists as a committee member in 1921.

Iranian border became extremely limited until the 1980s.

The Khrushchev Thaw

After Stalin died in 1953, control from Moscow became less severe under Nikita Khrushchev. Khrushchev was the head of the Communist Party from 1955 to 1964. This period, often referred to as the "Khrushchev Thaw," offered a greater tolerance for a wider range of literature, press, and scholarship. The Soviet Union also encouraged the manufacture of oil equipment in Azerbaijan to extract petroleum from its vast reserves. Since the 1960s, the Soviet Union came to depend on this Azerbaijani-built machinery. The oil wells in Baku flowed, and oil was transported by pipeline to Soviet Georgia.

Movements toward independence appeared in Azerbaijan but were quickly stopped. Khrushchev purged the leaders of the Azerbaijani Communist Party (ACP) in 1959 after suspicion of corruption and nationalism. Khrushchev's successor, Leonid I. Brezhnev, also removed ACP leadership for similar reasons, naming Heydar Aliyev the new chairman of the ACP in 1969. Aliyev had worked as a general for the KGB, the Communist secret police, but he secretly yearned for an independent Azerbaijan.

When Azerbaijan's oil reserves became depleted in the 1960s, Soviet investment in Azerbaijan decreased. Azerbaijan soon had the lowest economic growth rate of all the Soviet republics, while its population grew. Aliyev promoted alternative industries in Azerbaijan, which temporarily stimulated its economy. In 1982, Aliyev became a member of the Communist Party's politburo, or "political bureau," in Moscow, the highest position held by an Azerbaijani. Aliyev was forced to resign in 1987 by Mikhail Gorbachev, the Soviet president, because of his opposition to Gorbachev's reform policies, known as perestroika.

Nikita Sergeyevich Khrushchev (1894–1971), shown here when he was the Soviet premier, a post he held between 1958 and 1964, helped lead the USSR after the death of Joseph Stalin in 1953. Khrushchev effectively de-Stalinized the Union of Soviet Socialist Republics, putting an end to forced labor, the KGB secret police, and concentration camps.

The Struggle for Nationhood

The 1978 Islamic revolution in Iran had a profound impact on Azerbaijan, stimulating a religious revival there. Decades of religious repression by the Soviets made Islamic fundamentalism even more attractive to Azerbaijanis. This nationalistic spirit

This photograph of an oil worker adjusting a valve on a petroleum well in Baku was taken in 1957 during the period in which Azerbaijan was part of the USSR and under Soviet control. Soviet interest in Azerbaijan ebbed after its petroleum resources became depleted by the 1960s.

and interest in Islamic fundamentalism manifested itself in a renewed conflict with Azerbaijan's Christian Armenian population.

In 1988, ethnic violence broke out in Sumgait. Armenia was demanding reunification with Nagorno-Karabakh. Gorbachev tried to defuse the matter diplomatically but was forced to send Soviet troops to Baku to end the violence. Azerbaijanis resented the troops' presence, and organizations such as the Popular Front of Azerbaijan (PFA) gained

ground. It strove to capture political control from the Communists in Azerbaijan, but a split between conservative and moderate Muslims weakened its party.

The Karabakh incident, as well as other ethnic conflicts throughout the Soviet Union, led Communist leadership to believe that Gorbachev's reform politics gave the USSR's ethnic nationalities too much freedom. Conservative Communists staged a coup to oust Mikhail Gorbachev on August 19, 1991. The coup failed,

The Iranian Islamic Republican Army demonstrates in solidarity with people in the streets of Iran during the Iranian revolution. The posters are of the Ayatollah Khomeini, the Iranian religious and political leader.

leaving the USSR weak and unable to avoid the secession of republics from the Soviet Union. Azerbaijan became an independent nation on August 30, 1991. The final Communist Party chief, Ayaz N. Mutalibov, was elected president of the new Republic of Azerbaijan in September.

7 BIRTH OF A REPUBLIC

Political independence did not bring peace to the troubled region of Azerbaijan. Armenians living in Nagorno-Karabakh continued to demand either self-rule or reunification with Armenia. Azerbaijanis living in Nakhichevan also tore down barricades on the border with northern Iran to express their will to reunite with Azerbaijanis living there. In 1991, a full-fledged war broke out between Azerbaijan and Armenia. Armenians received better training than Azerbaijanis with the Soviet army and quickly gained the upper hand in the conflict. Armenians committed acts of genocide and ethnic cleansing against Azerbaijani civilians residing in Armenia. Ayaz Mutalibov's inability to raise a functioning army brought about his downfall, and he was forced to resign.

In June 1992, Popular Front leader Abulfaz Elchibey was elected president of Azerbaijan by a

GEORGIA

Ganja

NAGORNO

ARMENIA

Nakhichevan

This modern map of Azerbaijan shows the region divided by Armenia that borders the Azeri-speaking Iranian province called South Azerbaijan. Beginning the fight for independence, the Azerbaijan Soviet Socialist Republic rose up against the USSR in 1990 and endured a violent civil war with Armenia over Nagorno-Karabakh before gaining full independence from the Soviets in 1991.

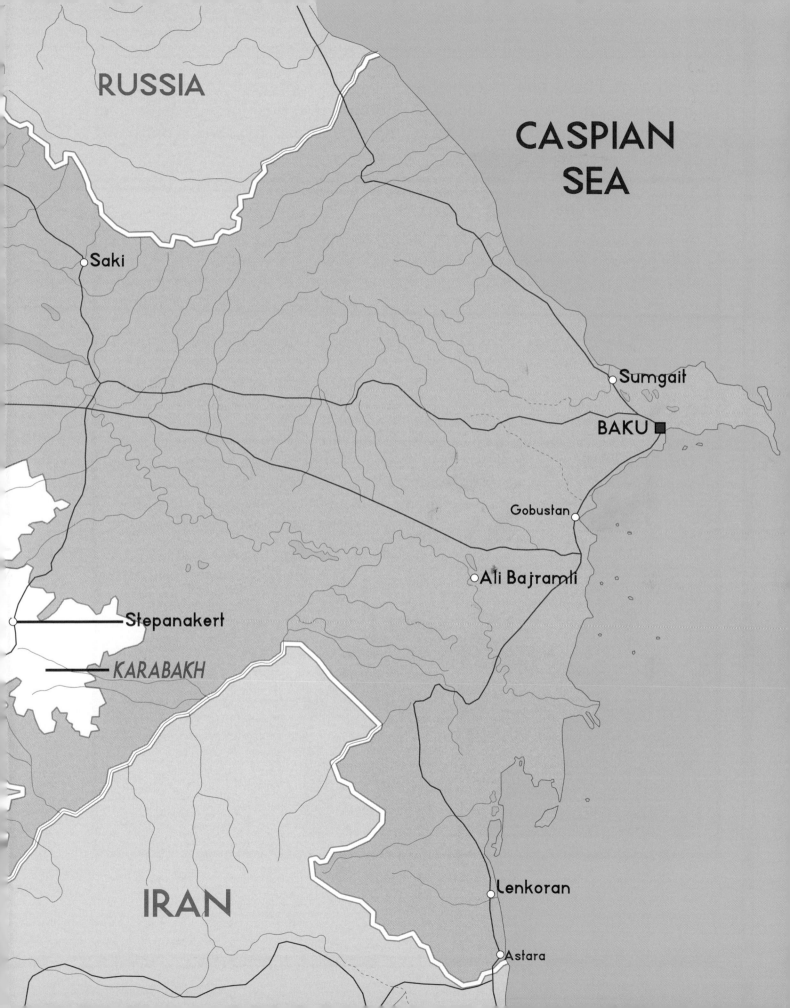

majority vote. He was a former political prisoner and dissident, stood for close relations with Turkey and Iran, and was opposed to joining the Commonwealth of Independent States. But he, too, was confronted

Nagorno-Karabakh

Despite a cease-fire agreement in the mid-1990s, the conflict continues between Azerbaijan and Armenia over the region known as Nagorno-Karabakh. This territory, which was once about 16 percent of Azerbaijan, is now largely Armenian populated and has created as many as one million Azerbaijani refugees, straining the nation's economy.

An independent region created in 1924 by the Soviet Union, Nagorno-Karabakh was at that time populated by nationalist Armenians seeking a separate sovereign state. By the 1960s, the Azerbaijani population was growing so rapidly that a conflict between these two peoples emerged. This conflict has, at times, become violent. In 1988, for instance, attacks between the two groups left hundreds dead. This violence was further complicated by Soviet involvement in the decision process about which group should govern the region. Between 1991 and 1993, fighting between Armenians and Azerbaijanis for increased territory caused the deaths of thousands on both sides, despite peace efforts by the United Nations and the Conference of Security and Cooperation in Europe. Today, Armenians occupy about one-fifth of the land claimed by the Republic of Azerbaijan.

The bombed-out building in this photograph is located in the Nagorno-Karabakh region of Azerbaijan, which was lost to Azerbaijan in 1994 after a bloody war with Armenia that started in 1991. At least 25,000 people died on both sides, and more than 700,000 Azerbaijanis fled the region and became refugees. The status of Nagorno-Karabakh is still in dispute by both nations.

This map shows the disputed region of Nagorno-Karabakh, an interior region of Azerbaijan shown on most contemporary maps of the country, which is currently controlled by Armenia.

Nagorno-Karabakh

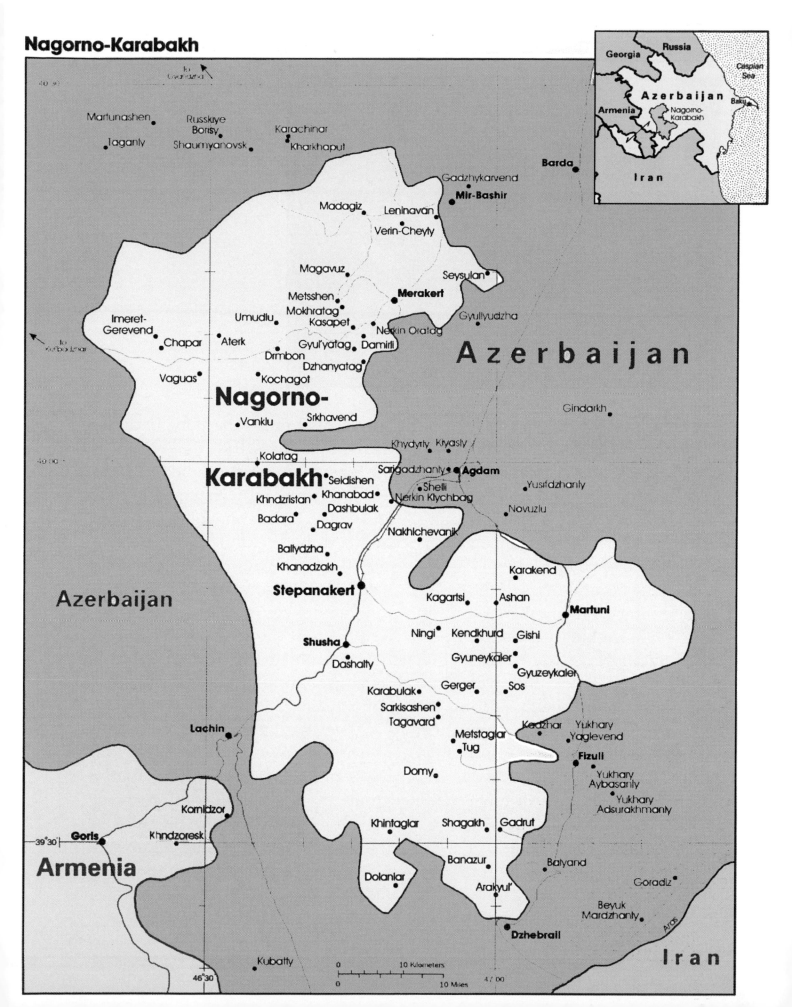

Martunashen •
Taganly •
Russkiye Borisy •
Shaumyanovsk •
Karachinar •
Kharkhaput •

Barda •

Gadzhykarvend •
Mir-Bashir •

Madagiz •
Leninavan •
Verin-Cheyly •

Seysulan •

Magavuz •

Metsshen •
Merakert •

Imeret-Gerevend •
Chapar •
Aterk •
Umudlu •
Mokhratag •
Kasapet •
Nerkin Oratag •

Gyullyudzha •

A z e r b a i j a n

Vaguas •
Drmbon •
Gyul'yatag •
Damirli •
Dzhanyatag •
Kochagot •

Gindarkh •

Nagorno-

Vanklu •
Srkhavend •

Karabakh
Seidishen •
Khydyrly •
Kiyasly •

Kolatag •
Sarigadzhanly •
Agdam •

Khndzristan •
Khanabad •
Shelli •
Yusifdzhanly •

Badara •
Dashbulak •
Nerkin Klychbag •

Dagrav •
Novuzlu •

Nakhichevanik •

Ballydzha •
Karakend •

Khanadzakh •

Stepanakert •
Kagartsi •
Ashan •

Ningi •
Kendkhurd •
Martuni •

Gishi •

A z e r b a i j a n

Shusha •
Gyuneykaler •

Dashalty •
Gyuzeykaler •

Gerger •
Sos •

Karabulak •

Sarkisashen •
Kedzhar •

Tagavard •
Yukhary Yaglevend •

Metstaglar •

Tug •
Fizuli •

Domy •
Yukhary Aybasanly •

Yukhary Adsurakhmanly •

Lachin •

Kornidzor •

Khintaglar •
Shagakh •
Gadrut •

Goris •
Khndzoresk •

Banazur •
Batyand •

Armenia
Dolanlar •
Goradiz •

Arakyul' •

Beyuk Mardzhanly •

Dzhebrail •

Iran

Kubatly •

0   10 Kilometers
0   10 Miles

To Gyandzha
To Kelbadzhar
Aros

President George W. Bush reaches out to shake the hand of the president of Azerbaijan, Heydar Aliyev, during their meeting in the White House Oval Office on February 26, 2003.

with the same problems as his predecessor, Mutalibov. Fighting in Nagorno-Karabakh turned to the Armenians' advantage after they seized about one-fifth of Azerbaijan's territory. More than a million Azerbaijani refugees then fled.

Elchibey found himself the object of a military rebellion in Ganja in June 1993. Lacking political support and facing a poor economy, Elchibey left Baku and went into hiding in Nakhichevan. Seizing the opportunity to make a political comeback, the former Communist Party leader Heydar Aliyev was elected president in October 1993. This election was boycotted by Elchibey's Popular Front.

President Aliyev brought relative stability and economic growth to Azerbaijan. He is credited with stop-ping armed mobs that have roamed the streets since the dissolution of the Soviet Union. He signed a cease-fire agreement with Armenia in 1994 and halted the bloodshed, which by then had claimed more than 20,000 lives. Unfortunately, Karabakh Armenians again declared independence in 1999. Nagorno-Karabakh is now an independent region with ties to Armenia, but it remains a conflict between the two nations.

Aliyev has faced several coups but remains in power. In 1994, he signed the "Contract of the Century" with a group of international oil corporations to explore offshore oil fields in the Caspian Sea. Since 1998, Aliyev's New Azerbaijan Party claims the majority of seats in the Milli Majlis, Azerbaijan's national assembly,

Azerbaijanis buy and sell vegetables and fruits in this open-air market in Baku. The economy of Baku is changing, recently making progress for the first time since the Soviet era. The overall economic structure of Azerbaijan, again made profitable since offshore drilling of petroleum in the Caspian Sea began in the late 1990s, depends largely on the demand for oil and its changing price in the global economy.

though some Azerbaijanis have been advocating for Aliyev's removal due to his political monopoly. In 2001, the Republic of Azerbaijan became a member of the Council of Europe, a collective of nations endorsing human rights and due process of law.

Today, Azerbaijan's standard of living is low by Western standards. However, foreign investment in the oil industry may jump-start its economy, which still suffers the repercussions caused by the violent conflict with Armenia.

TIMELINE

900 BC Kingdom of Manna is founded in southern Azerbaijan.

800 BC Scythians invade from the Black Sea and north Caucasus.

628 BC The prophet Zoroaster is born in Persia.

550 BC Cyrus the Great ousts King Astyages and expands the Achaemenid Empire.

331 BC Alexander the Great defeats Darius III, then invades Azerbaijan.

66 BC Romans invade Azerbaijan.

AD 226 Sassanid dynasty is established; *Zend Avesta* codifies Zoroastrian religion.

313 Constantine declares Christianity the official religion of Byzantine Empire.

642 The Arab caliphate invades Azerbaijan, introducing Islam.

816–837 Babak leads insurrections against Arab caliphate in Caucasian Albania.

880s–990s Autonomous feudal states form in Azerbaijan.

1051 Beginning of the Seljuk invasion of Azerbaijan.

1136 Creation of the Atabek state of Azerbaijan under Shams ad-din Ildeniz.

1387 Timur the Great conquers Persia.

1453 Ottoman Turks seize Constantinople.

1468 The Aq-Qoyunlu control Azerbaijan.

1501 Safavid Empire created in Azerbaijan under Shah Ismail I.

1722 Peter the Great of Russia invades Baku to secure Caspian Sea access.

1739 Reign of Nadir Shah; end of Safavid dynasty.

1813 Treaty of Gulistan signed between Russia and Persia.

1838 Treaty of Turkmanchay gives Armenian territory to Russia.

1912 Musavat Party forms to fight for Azerbaijani freedom.

1914 World War I erupts in Europe.

1917 Czar Nicholas II is overthrown; Bolshevik revolution in Russia begins.

1918 Azerbaijan People's Democratic Republic declares itself as autonomous state.

1920 Red Army invades Azerbaijan.

1922 Transcaucasian Federated Soviet Socialist Republic of the USSR is formed.

1926 Joseph Stalin rules the Soviet Union.

1936 Transcaucasian Federated Soviet Socialist Republic of the USSR disbands.

1939 World War II breaks out; Russia suffers catastrophic losses.

1941 Red Army invades Iran, then is forced to withdraw by Western Allies in 1946.

1955 Nikita Khrushchev becomes leader of the Soviet Communist Party.

1969 Heydar Aliyev becomes head of the Azerbaijani Communist Party.

1978 Islamic revolution in Iran.

1988 Ethnic violence breaks out in Nagorno-Karabakh.

1991 Collapse of the Soviet Union; Azerbaijan becomes an independent republic.

1992 War between Armenia and Azerbaijan over control of Nagorno-Karabakh.

1993 President Elchibey is replaced by Heydar Aliyev for failing to halt the violence.

1994 Cease-fire agreement brings peace between Azerbaijan and Armenia.

1998 Heydar Aliyev re-elected president.

1999 Armenia declares Nagorno-Karabakh an autonomous Armenian territory.

2001 Azerbaijan provides assistance to the United States after terrorist attacks.

2002 Construction begins on a pipeline to carry oil from the Caspian Sea to Turkey.

2003 Offshore drilling of petroleum in the Capsian Sea continues to help improve the standard of living for Azerbaijanis.

GLOSSARY

abdicate To renounce power.

Bolshevik A member of the extremist wing of the Russian Social Democratic Party that seized power in Russia during the revolution of November 1917.

Caucasia (Transcaucasia) A region in southeastern Europe between the Black and Caspian Seas divided by the Caucasus Mountains including Russia, Georgia, Azerbaijan, and Armenia.

Cold War A conflict of ideological differences carried on without full military action and usually without breaking up diplomatic relationships. A condition of rivalry and mistrust between countries, as with the United States and the Union of Soviet Socialist Republics in the mid- to late twentieth century.

Communism A political system that advocates the elimination of private property; a system in which all goods are owned by the people and are divided among them equally.

coup (coup d'état) A French term meaning "blow to the state," referring to a sudden, unexpected overthrow of a government by outsiders.

Cyrillic The script in which Russian is written.

czar A ruler of Russia until the 1917 revolution.

dissident A person who disagrees with political or religious systems, organizations, or beliefs.

enclave A distinct territory enclosed within or as if within a foreign territory.

Hellenism Devotion to or imitation of ancient Greek thought and customs.

imperialism The policy or practice by a nation to exert power over another country's territory and/or to gain control over that country and its resources indirectly, often to the point of exploitation.

Islam The religious faith of Muslims.

Milli Majlis The national assembly of Azerbaijan.

monotheistic A type of religion that worships one god.

Muslim A person who worships Allah and follows the Islamic faith.

nationalism Loyalty and devotion to a nation, placing an emphasis on its culture above others.

perestroika Mikhail Gorbachev's program of economic, political, and social restructuring that became the prime motivator for the destabilization of the totalitarian Soviet Union.

politburo A Russian word meaning political bureau; the executive organization for a number of Communist Parties.

Shia A sect of Islam that supports the claim of Ali and his line and their presumptive right to the caliphate and leadership of the Muslim community.

Shiite A Muslim of the Shia branch or sect of Islam.

Stalinism The political, economic, and social principles and policies associated with Stalin, especially the theory and practice of Communism developed by Stalin from Marxism.

Sunni A division or sect of Islam that adheres to a traditional form of the religion and respects the first four caliphs as rightful successors of Muhammad; the largest sect of Islam.

Union of Soviet Socialist Republics (USSR) The Soviet Union that existed between 1922 and 1991 and was comprised of territory between eastern Europe and northern Asia.

Zoroastrianism A monotheistic Persian religion founded in the sixth century BC by the prophet Zoroaster.

FOR MORE INFORMATION

Embassy of the Republic of Azerbaijan
2741 34th Street NW
Washington, DC 20008
(202) 337–3500
Web site: http://www.azembassy.com

Web Sites
Due to the changing nature of Internet links, the Rosen Publishing Group, Inc., has developed an online list of Web sites related to the subject of this book. This site is updated regularly. Please use this link to access the list:

http://www.rosenlinks.com/liha/azer

FOR FURTHER READING

Croissant, Michael P. *The Armenia-Azerbaijan Conflict: Causes and Implications.* Westport, CT: Praeger Publishers, 1998.

Goltz, Thomas. *Azerbaijan Diary: A Rogue Reporter's Adventures in an Oil-Rich, War-Torn Post-Soviet Republic.* Armonk, NY: M. E. Sharpe, Inc., 1998.

Heyat, Farideh. *Azeri Women in Transition: Women in Soviet and Post-Soviet Azerbaijan.* New York: Routledge, 2002.

Swietochowski, Tadeusz, and Brian C. Collins. *Historical Dictionary of Azerbaijan.* Blue Ridge Summit, PA: Scarecrow Press, Inc., 1999.

Van Der Leeuw, Charles. *Azerbaijan: A Quest for Identity.* New York: St. Martin's Press, 1998.

BIBLIOGRAPHY

Armenia, Azerbaijan, and Georgia Country Studies. Area handbook series. Washington, DC: Federal Research Division, Library of Congress, 1995.

Roberts, Elizabeth. *Georgia, Armenia, and Azerbaijan.* Brookfield, CT: Millbrook Press, 1992.

Suny, Ronald Grigor. *The Baku Commune, 1917–1918: Class and Nationality in the Russian Revolution.* Princeton, NJ: Princeton University Press, 1972.

Swietochowski, Tadeusz. *Russian Azerbaijan, 1905–1920: The Shaping of National Identity in a Muslim Community.* New York: Cambridge University Press, 1985.

Werner, Lewis, "Roots Deeper than Oil." *Aramco World,* January/February 2000, pp. 2–11.

Van Der Leeuw, Charles. *Azerbaijan: A Quest for Identity.* New York: St. Martin's Press, 1998.

INDEX

About the Author

Sherri Liberman is a freelance author who lives in New York City.

Acknowledgement

Special thanks to Karin van der Tak for her expert guidance regarding matters pertaining to the Middle East and Asia.

Photo Credits

Cover (foreground map), pp. 1 (foreground), 4–5, 54–55 © 2002 Geoatlas; cover (background map), pp. 1 (background), 16–17, 20, 32–33, 35, 40, 57 courtesy of the General Libraries, the University of Texas at Austin; cover (top left), pp. 6, 24 © Trip/N & J Wiseman; cover (bottom left), p. 58 © AP/Wide World Photos; cover (bottom right), p. 40 (inset) © Sotheby's/AKG; © pp. 8–9, 10, 12–13, 19, 22–23, 25, 26, 28–29, 36, 48–49 maps designed by Tahara Hasan; p. 9 (right) © Roshanak B./Corbis Sygma; p. 11 © Art Archive Museum/Museum of Anatolian Civilisations, Ankara/Dagli Orti; pp. 14, 59 © Trip/V Slapinia; pp. 15, 18 © Archivo Iconografico, S.A./Corbis; p. 21 © AKG; p. 29 (inset) © Stapleton Collection/Corbis; p. 30 © Bursein Collection/Corbis; p. 31 © Roger Wood/Corbis; pp. 38, 53 © Hulton/Archive/Getty Images; pp. 42, 51 © Bettmann/Corbis; pp. 43, 44, 45, 46, 50 © Mary Evans Picture Library; p. 52 © Yevgeny Khaldei/Corbis; p. 56 © David Turnley/Corbis.

Designer: Tahara Hasan; **Editor:** Joann Jovinelly; **Photo Researcher:** Elizabeth Loving